I Was Just

THINKING

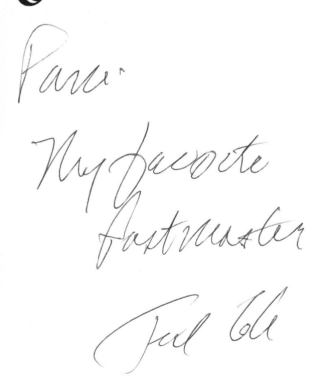

TED COLE

ISBN 978-1-0980-1872-6 (paperback)
ISBN 978-1-0980-1873-3 (digital)

Christian Faith Publishing, Inc.
832 Park Avenue
Meadville, PA 16335
www.christianfaithpublishing.com

Printed in the United States of America

ALL HALLOWS EVE

B ack in the eighth century, Pope Gregory III designated November 1 as a day for honoring saints and martyrs. The evening before was known as "All Hallows Eve," now Halloween. The Celts believed that on All Hallows Eve, more so than any other time of the year, the ghosts of the dead were able to mingle with the living because the souls of those who had died during the year traveled into the otherworld. People gathered to sacrifice animals, fruits, and vegetables. They also lit bonfires, in honor of the dead, to aid them on their journey and to keep them away from the living, attempting to scare them away by wearing masks. On that day, all manner of beings were abroad—ghosts, fairies, demons, and all parts of the dark and dread.

At the end of October, the church observes All Saints Day when we honor those members of our church family who have died during the year. Why honor the dead? Because they are family. There is enough ritual that takes place during worship on Sunday mornings that we don't always recognize acts that identify us as a family. In my mind, the sanctuary is the equivalent of a dining room. Do you see the table? When we sit in the pews, we are really sitting on dining room chairs. We are sitting at the Lord's table. Every worship service is a meal where we share the bread of God's word—read, taught, and preached—and we drink the wine of God's blessing.

In the Jewish synagogue service, they have a practice of naming the names of those who have died during the week, and at the end of the year, the list for the whole year is read and special prayers offered. When do we normally memorialize the dead? At Easter with the lilies. At Christmas with the poinsettias. When we dedicate organs, choir robes and hymnals. It becomes an economic consideration, sometimes. We remember those who can pay for it.

There is a reason why, in some Christian funeral services, the casket is covered with a pall. The reason is because in a real family, no distinction is made between family members: there is no difference between a pine box and a Cadillac model. Did you know that in a Moravian cemetery, all the headstones are the same? The other thing is that they are buried in a family plot. We bury our loved ones in a communal plot—scattered and alone. I am thinking that if we as the church are family while we are alive, why shouldn't we be family when we are dead?

Bad Table Manners

There is a right and wrong way to eat, according to those who know about these things. According to Emily Post, the fork and napkin go to the left of the plate while the spoon and knife go to the right. And by the way, you never put the fork on the napkin, and the cutting edge of the knife always faces the plate. The drinking glass goes at two o'clock above the plate, while the bread plate with a butter knife when used goes at ten o'clock. It is rude for men to wear their hat while eating. Reading the newspaper is permissible only at the breakfast table. If, for some reason, you must spit food out, you spit it into the napkin and place the napkin on your lap—*not on the table*. Food is to be passed around the table counter-clockwise. Chew with your mouth closed. Excuse yourself from the table if you have to blow your nose. Don't pick your teeth. Don't put your elbows on the table. Don't reach across the table for anything—ask that it be passed. And there are particularly rude noises that have no place at the dinner table.

My guess is that many modern families do not use dinner tables since the invention of the TV tray, and couches serve as both table and chair. So, when it comes to eating at home, etiquette has gone by the way of the dinosaur.

In the church of Paul's day, Holy Communion was combined with a covered dish dinner called a love feast. Everyone brought a casserole and it was passed around the table home-style. Originally, the altar table of the Lord's Supper was much bigger than it is now. At the end of the meal, the bread and the cup were blessed and served, "This is my body, broken for you. This is my blood, shed for your sins." The problem was, the more well-to-do members of the church had no table manners. They would arrive early, eat, drink, and be merry; and by the time the less fortunate arrived, there would be nothing left to eat. This helps explain what Paul meant when he said to the Corinthians, "Whoever, therefore, eats the bread or drinks the cup of the Lord in an unworthy manner will be answerable for the body and blood of the Lord... For all who eat and drink without discerning the body, eat and drink judgment against themselves." Discerning the body means being inclusive. Some were eating and drinking while excluding others. Then when it came time to participate in the Lord's Supper—a communal meal—these early arrivers were going through the motions of being inclusive. What I mean to suggest is that when it comes to eating at the Lord's table, there is a right and wrong way to eat. If, in our hearts, we have excluded anyone, judged anyone, labeled anyone, condemned anyone—and receive the bread and cup—it's bad table manners and downright rude. It's not church.

Baggage

We used to do a lot of tent camping back when our bones were less brittle. Our neighbors must have gotten a lot of pleasure out of watching us pack the van. There was the tent, of course, and the poles, stakes, screen porch, camp lanterns, pots and pans, water jug, sleeping bags, pillows, blankets, air mattresses, hair dryer, food, suitcases, raincoats, first aid kit, clothes line, mosquito repellent, hot dog sticks, lawn chairs, Tupper ware, weather scanner, and an electric blanket. Electric blanket? "Why are we taking an electric blanket?" I asked the wife.

"In case it gets cold."

"But we have the sleeping bags and thirty-two blankets! And besides, what if we camp where there is no electricity?"

"That's why we are taking a portable generator," says wife.

"I'm going to pack a hard hat."

The wife replied, "Why a hard hat?"

I said, "In case there is an earthquake!"

I know you've been there. It takes a camping trip to realize just how much stuff you cram into your life—what we consider important. We are overpacked and overstuffed. I mention this because one of the characteristics of the early Christians was they traveled light. "Take no gold, silver, or copper, no bag for your journey, not more than one tunic, not more than one pair of sandals—just the clothes on your back." Sounds pretty austere and not very practical—especially if you are going camping. But of course, Jesus isn't talking about camping or taking a trip to Disney. He's talking about *the* journey.

It's the journey we all take when we signed up from the moment of our baptism.

I'm not a fan of creeds and doctrines, and they have their place. But the further along I go down this dusty road of discipleship, the less need I have for a systematic theology. Yet there are churches out there that are making people jump through hoops, loading them down with doctrinal paraphernalia. It really doesn't take that much stuff to get God's attention. When it comes to that, less is more, and more is less.

Being Meek Is Not
What You Think

In the late 1600s, the magnificent St. Paul's Cathedral in London was built by the famous architect, Sir Christopher Wren. When it was finished, he took the king of England on a tour of the structure. The king's response was, "This cathedral is amusing, awful, and artificial." Sir Christopher Wren was delighted. Because back then, "amusing" meant "amazing," "awful" meant "awesome," and "artificial" meant "artistic."

Words change their meaning over time. Take the word, "bad." When I was growing up, you were bad if you spray painted your sister's gym shoes or broke curfew. Today, however, you are bad if you are suave and debonair. If a teenager says that something is "cool," he/she means that it's "hot." There was a time when you could use the word "gay," to describe someone who was lighthearted and carefree. Not anymore. There are a number of words in the Bible that get misinterpreted or misapplied. Jesus once said, "Suffer the children to come to me." Suffer the children? "Though I speak with the tongues of men and of angels, and have not charity, I am become as sounding brass or a tinkling cymbal." You offer someone charity these days, and they are offended. "Blessed are the meek, for they shall inherit the earth."

What do you think of when you hear the word "meek"? I think of someone who is passive, conforming, weak-minded, soft-spoken, and compliant. A dishrag. A milksop. What is the virtue in being meek? Here is one of those words that the writers of the King James

Version of the Bible used in sixteenth century England that takes on a completely different meaning for modern readers. At the time, the word made sense in its context. The word, "meek," comes from the word, "mucus." That's right—that stuff that comes out of your nose when you sneeze. Mucus is the slowest moving fluid in the body. So, to be meek is to be slow in our reaction to aggression, slow to anger, slow to criticize, slow to draw conclusions, and slow to judge. When Jesus said, "Blessed are the meek," he was blessing those who could control their emotions. Meekness, after all, is not a weakness but a strength—for to refuse to react or give in to pressure takes a lot of strength.

There is a telling scene in the movie, *To Kill a Mockingbird*. Atticus is a lawyer in the south before the Civil War who is defending a black man accused of raping a white girl, and the man is condemned by an all-white jury. After the trial, Atticus goes to the family of the condemned man to assure them that he will appeal. While he is talking to the family, the alcoholic father of the girl that was raped walked up to Atticus and spit in his face. There is a dramatic lull in the action as the two stare at each other, the spittle dripping down Atticus's face. Finally, Atticus pulls out a handkerchief, wipes his face, gets into his car, and drives away. I guess Atticus was woose, a weakling, and a pushover. No, he was meek.

Between Sixes and Sevens

My neighbor, Brian, has been cutting my grass while recovering from recent surgery. He's a good Joe, but lately, he has been in a grump. "What's going on?" I asked.

"Well, as you know we spent gazillion dollars to put in a sand mound septic system, and it's already backing up. Then yesterday, while driving home from work, my truck broke down five miles from home. Then when I was changing brake pads on the truck, I whacked my thumb at it hurts like ****."

"Wow!" said I.

"Yeah wow," he said. "You're the preacher. Is God out to get me?"

It's no accident that the poetry in Genesis describes creation as a six-day event. The world is a six and everything in it. This helps to explain why things are so apt to go awry, why there is sickness, violence, and disappointment—and sewer backups. Only God is a seven. But if I read the creation story correctly, the lesson is that there will be a seventh day—a day when everything turns into a seven.

I went to visit a parishioner farmer who was having a particularly difficult time. His best milking cow died. It was a wet summer, and he was unable to bale as much hay as last year. He wrenched his back while shoveling manure. After a long list of bad luck, he said to me, "I am between sixes and sevens."

I never heard that expression before, but it made sense in a number of ways. To be between perfection and imperfection—isn't that where we all are? It's the human condition. Living in an imperfect world is not easy, especially when we are looking for miracles, for sevens. But I look at it this way, God could have created a perfect world. But what if God, in his infinite wisdom, decided that a seven-type world would be a disaster? It would be a disaster because in a perfect world, there would be no room for love. I mean, after all, isn't it love that makes things perfect?

CHARIS

For Christmas several years ago, someone gave me a machine that duplicates sounds of nature. I was having trouble sleeping nights, and my friend thought that this gift would cure my insomnia. It has six settings—heartbeat, spring rain, mountain stream, white noise, ocean waves, and summer night. You can set a timer for fifteen, thirty, and forty-five minutes, and there is a volume control. I tried each of the sounds on different nights, and it was an exercise in futility. I had the heartbeat on for five minutes, and I truly believed I was going to have a heart attack. The spring rain setting reminded me of a leaky roof, and I was under the leak. The mountain stream made me go to the bathroom. The white noise reminded me of radio static, the ocean waves made me sea sick, and the cricket on the summer night sounded more like the tick of a clock.

I am thinking about those gifts we get for Christmas—the proverbial tie, the pink and brown afghan Aunt Thelma made, and the vegetable slicer/dicer—all ending up in a dark corner of the cupboard or broom closet. I know it's true that it's the thought that counts, but then I say, "What were they thinking!" What is it about a gift that sometimes it does not rise to the standard of "gift?" What constitutes a gift? There is the dictionary definition, "Something voluntarily transferred by one person to another without expectation of compensation."

If Aunt Thelma comes to your house, does not see her afghan draped over the living room sofa, and says, "Where's the afghan I got you for Christmas?" then the afghan has suddenly lost its "giftness" and has become a bribe. Unwittingly, sometimes, we offer people gifts that are loaded with conditions and quid pro quo. True giving is such a rare thing because a gift by nature is something offered without strings attached. That's what Jesus meant when he said, "When you give, don't be like the hypocrites who love to draw attention to their gift." The setting for this warning is a stage. "When you pray, give or fast," says Jesus, "don't be like actors on stage who are looking for an applause or a thank you." He goes on to say, "When you give, don't let your left hand know what the right hand is doing!" In other words, if you need an audience when you give to the poor, it's not a gift. Only when it is given in secret, when you are not looking for a "thank you," does it rise to the level of true giving.

The New Testament word for "grace" is *charis,* which is translated "gift." When Paul says we are saved by grace, through faith, he is saying that salvation is a gift. It cannot be earned. It is not deserved. Why, then, when the church offers salvation to the world, is it loaded with conditions? You are saved, if…we make salvation conditional sometimes because even Christians who ought to know better cannot believe that Jesus's love does not come with strings attached. But this distinction is what makes God's love for us so different from our love for God. We love God because we're looking for something. God loves us because he has already found it. The gospel writer, John, makes it very clear, "God so loved the world that he *gave* his only son." I am thinking that if John meant to suggest God's love for the world is anything other than a gift, he would have used a different word!

God's gift of Christ to the world is our standard for what it means to give and to receive. We can only approximate that kind of giving because buried beneath all that good will that surfaces during the Christmas season, there is our need for applause, for recognition, and for acknowledgement. Jane Merchant was reflecting on what it means to give—let me share it with you:

> Whatever gift I give to you is yours. Give it
> away, or keep it, as you will.
> The special books, the china miniatures,
> The little birds carved with beguiling
> skill—I shall not peer about your house to see

If they are dusted well and duly shown
To visitors, as treasured things may be; I
made a gift of them, and not a loan.
I know that even gifts sincerely loved
Both for themselves and for the giver's sake
Save in life's many changes often proved
A burden; be relieved of the mistake
Of thinking you must keep a gift I give
(Except my love) as long as you shall live.

CHICKEN BOOTS

There was a man in our church named Fort Kline. Fort lived alone in a large house on the edge of town that he inherited from his mother when she died. He never married because he spent the better part of his adult life taking care of his invalid mother. When he was in his early fifties, he had a stroke, which left the left side of his face paralyzed. For this reason, he couldn't keep spit in his mouth, and it always ran down that corner and onto his chin. His speech was mumbled, and you had to listen carefully to understand him. He had a habit of inserting "you know" at the end of every phrase, but it would come out "no" because he couldn't pronounce his y's. But most people simply ignored him, rather than watch the spit dribble down his chin and try to decode his speech. But that didn't keep Fort from coming to church, and it didn't dampen his spirits. He was always smiling, going out of his way to shake everyone's hand. Fort raised chickens and sold eggs and poultry. When he came to church, he always wore what I called his "chicken boots," which disgusted everyone. He loved children and donated all the eggs and candy for the Easter egg hunt every year. When the choir had a fundraiser to buy new choir robes, Fort paid for them with his "chicken" money.

Fort played an important role at the children's Christmas pageant one year. There was a large bed sheet draped across a wire, and after everyone sang a verse of "Away in a Manger," a little boy dressed in a centurion's outfit stepped out from behind the bed sheet to open the show, "In those days a decree went out from Caesar Augustus that all the world should be taxed…" Then the bed sheet was pulled back to reveal Mary and Joseph, two shepherds in bathrobes, the sheep in their cotton balls, and a star made of cardboard wrapped in tinfoil, dangling on a wire above. And then a makeshift spotlight focused on the baby Jesus in a cradle, a doll wrapped in a baby blanket. The centurion returned and picked up where he left off, "And while they were there, the time came for her to be delivered. And she gave birth to her first-born son, wrapped him in swaddling clothes, and laid him in a manger."

Every now and then—when we try to bring the sacred and the secular together—it actually happens. No one really expects a children's pageant to do much more than give parents and grandparents the pleasure of oohing and aahing at the children—with their cardboard angel wings, tilted halos, worn out bath robes, stumbling over their lines—reenact Christmas. A draped bed sheet, a makeshift star, and a doll are a far cry from Hollywood, so imagination is a critical prop for these pageants. On this particular occasion, it was when Mary picked up the Christ child, in the middle of singing "Silent Night," that the smell hit the room. It was Fort's chicken boots and the smell of barn. We couldn't produce a real manger—real sheep, real cattle, real donkeys—but we could produce the smell. Put that smell together with a grin from a toothless chicken farmer, and you have the makings of a real Christmas.

Christmas Outsiders

"I saw three ships come sailing in." Who were these wise guys—the Wise Men, the Magi, the Kings—who came to visit the Christ child? Their story is found only in Matthew who tells us that they came from the "east." The east was likely Persia or modern-day Iran. The religion of ancient Persia was Zoroastrian, a religion that practiced a kind of cosmic dualism where the god of the spirit world was always in conflict with the god of the material world. This conflict is lived out in the lives of humans where the two gods compete for their souls. It was believed that the heavenly bodies provided insight into the spiritual truths, which are needed to assure oneself of eternal life. And so, people relied on astrologers to help them discern these spiritual truths. For this reason, it is thought that Matthew's wise men were indeed astrologers who saw the unusually bright star to the west. Such a phenomenon would have been an omen to these astrologers that something of cosmic importance was about to take place. Why they thought it was the birth of a king, Matthew does not tell us.

So, they packed up their camels, and off they went following the star that hovered over Bethlehem. God gave a sign to a group of truth seekers who were likely not Jews, that is, outsiders. Here's a side of the Christmas story we often miss.

God doesn't speak only to Christians, and isn't that what is going on here—God making use of those who don't subscribe to the insider's version of how God thinks? The Wise Men, for me, represent those in our community who are seeking spiritual truths but may be considered "outsiders" by our standards.

John records an episode in which a group of Greeks—outsiders—have come to worship at the Jewish Passover. They came to Philip and asked if they could meet Jesus. Philip went and told Andrew, and together they went and told Jesus. Jesus says, "The hour has come for the Son of Man to be glorified." The Wise Men—outsiders—arrive to honor the beginning of Jesus's life, and it is the Gentiles—outsiders—who have come to signal the arrival of Jesus's final days.

The next time you get a Christmas card showing Jesus in a manger, flanked by Mary and Joseph, take time to consider who else were there—shepherds and Zoroastrian priests—outsiders. When it comes to the kingdom of God, there is no "us" and "them."

Chronos and Kairos

You are sitting in your lazy boy in the living room, looking out the window—watching. You get up, go to the window, pull back the curtain, survey the street in front of the house, and return to your chair. You try not to notice that it is after midnight, and your daughter is still not home from the basketball game. A car slows down, you rush to the window—it is not your daughter. It is going on 1:00 a.m. and the phone rings. "Mom, Danny's car broke down—we had to have it towed to the garage. I thought I better call—I know you would be worried."

How long does it take for your daughter to come home? An eternity. We are talking about two different times, aren't we? There is the time on the clock above the mantel, and there is the time that is ticking in your heart. The one is *chronos* time, the other is *kairos* time.

My students in Disciple have gotten used to my harping about the difference between *chronos* time and *kairos* time. *Chronos* time is the time on our clocks and calendars—it is the seconds, minutes, hours, days, years, and eons. *Chronos* is the time it takes for the sun to rise and set and the moon to run its lunar cycle. It's the time it takes to recover from surgery. *Chronos* time describes the impact that cause and effect have on our life, a sense that things happen sequentially and logically. We are *chromos*-oriented. We expect certain things to occur *in due time*.

But there are events that occur in our lives that do not subscribe to *chronos* time. *Kairos* is the time it takes for a GI in Afghanistan to receive a letter from home. It's the expectant father, pacing the floor of the hospital visiting room. It's the time it takes for a broken heart to heal and the time it takes for one to forgive and be forgiven. It's the time God uses to get things done.

We are interested in time while God is interested in the timely. You are hanging out at the mall with your guy friends, and you see a woman pass by who is clearly overweight. Her hair is a mess, and her clothes disheveled. One of your friends comments as she passes by, "Look at that disaster!" And you laugh. You know that he spoke loud enough for the woman to hear, and you know she is not laughing. You recall in Ecclesiastes, where it says, "There is a time to laugh," and you know instinctively that this was not the time. It's a *kairos* thing.

When is the best time to love someone? Your watch cannot tell you that! These kinds of things operate outside the laws of cause and effect. They sneak up on us without warning, with no apparent logic or reason. There are things that happen that are not controlled by the tick of a clock. The difference between *chronos* time and *kairos* time is the difference between how we see and do things and the way God sees and does things. We have to learn to listen to the tick of a different clock if we want to know God.

There are a number of Christians who are preoccupied with the time of Jesus's return. They are turning to Daniel and the book of Revelation to predict the end of the world. But Jesus coming is not a *chronos* event so much as it is a *kairos* event. If we are looking for Jesus in *chronos* time, a date on the calendar, we will likely miss him because Jesus coming is a man sleeping on a park bench, his coming is a choir singing Handel's *Messiah, and* his coming is two or three or more gathered to pray and listen to the Word. He appears as a thief in the night when we least expect it. He can appear in a loaf of bread and a cup of wine. December 25 is not Christmas—Christmas is an encounter with the man who calmed the sea and hung on a cross.

D = I + P

It is necessary for us, on occasion, to ask, "What are we up to? Why do we occupy this corner of the world?" We are learning that church as we knew it fifty years ago, is no longer relevant, that there is a significant number of young people—the millennials—who are not interested in "church as usual." We are told that they are not interested in doctrines or creeds—things that were of utmost important to me when I was their age. They are interested in Christ but not in Christianity. Should we change with the times or should we hold on to our traditions?

It may surprise many of us that since the church's birth at Pentecost—the mission of the church is not to get people to believe and belong—but to become disciples. That is, what happens to the seed after it has been planted?

I have performed many weddings, and in almost every case, the couple brings their list—who is the maid of honor? Who is the best man? What will the bridesmaids be wearing? Will the bride be holding a bouquet? Who will give her away? What about the reception? Shall the bride use a train? Will there be a runner? What about a candelabra? Pastor, can my dog be the ring bearer?

After they are done with their list, I ask them, "What is most important to you right now—the wedding or the marriage?" And they look at me as if I had two heads. "Well, we hadn't thought of that." What do you do after the seed has been planted?

I am not sure why, but many Christians think of faith as a noun rather than a verb. It's about belonging to a church. It's about believing in the virgin birth or reciting the Apostle's Creed. Being a Christian is about believing and belonging. Christians are being taught rather than teaching, they are still following when they should be leading, they are still leaning when they should be lifting, and they are still looking to be blessed when they should be a blessing.

I know that being inspired and getting warm fuzzies is important for a lot of people. But it's not so much what you know in your head, nor what you feel in your heart that makes you a disciple. but what you become.

I am not saying that learning and warm fuzzies are not important. The question is, it's not so much what you know in your head, nor what you feel in your heart that makes you a disciple—it's what you become. $D=I+P$. Disciple = Inspiration + Perspiration. This what it takes to get the seed to grow.

DANDELIONS

I mentioned my neighbor who has this thing about Christians—he doesn't like them. He also has a thing about dandelions. I have this ongoing debate with him regarding the dandelion. I say it's a flower; he says it's a weed. When I cut grass in late spring. I feel like I am cutting down a flowerbed, the yard is so full of dandelions. My neighbor's sentiments are just the opposite—he can't wait to get rid of those "weeds" cluttering his lawn. So, we go back and forth, "It's a flower!"

"No, it's a blasted weed!"

So, I went and Googled the dandelion to see if I could bolster my point of view, and this is what I learned. First of all, it was not until the twentieth century that dandelions were considered a weed. Before that, they were considered a great source of food, medicine, and magic. In fact, gardeners used to weed out the grass to make room for the dandelions!

The practical purposes of the dandelion are well documented—it serves as a gentle diuretic, it removes toxins from the blood stream; aids the kidneys; the leaves are more nutritious than lettuce as a salad; has more vitamin C than tomatoes and higher in iron, potassium, and calcium than one-a-day tablets; their wide-spreading roots aid in loosening the soil to allow for healthier grass; and dandelion tea is a marvelous tonic that aids in digestion of food. Shall I mention the beautiful flowers they produce—bright yellow that compliments the green grass? And we want to kill it!

But perhaps the most endearing quality of the dandelion is its toughness. It will grow up through concrete! In fact, the "flower" is

French—*dent de lion*—"lion's teeth." It has learned to survive in all environments and conditions. Maybe this is why I have a fondness for the dandelion. I don't eat the plant. I just admire its beauty and tenacity.

But faced with these facts my neighbor has not changed his mind. He has it in his head that dandelions are a menace. I asked him why he hates dandelions so much. He said, "Because they are there!" Sounds like something Hitler may have said about the Jews, something Osama Bin Laden said about the US, or something George Wallace said about the blacks. When it comes down to it, my neighbor doesn't need a reason to hate anything or anybody—dandelions, Christians, or Republicans. I guess when it comes to hate and prejudice, we don't need a reason. The fact that people we don't like are there is reason enough.

Do You Love Me?

I like the cartoon showing Adam and Eve walking hand in hand in the garden. Eve is in a particularly romantic mood. "Do you love me?" she asks Adam. Adams says the only thing he can say. "Who else?" Donna will say to me, "Ted, do you love me?" And I want to say, "Who else?" But I know what she is asking. She's asking, "How much?"

More than the other gospel writers, John is aware of his audience, those Christians who will be reading and hearing this gospel as they gather for worship. In almost every verse, there is a message hidden behind innuendo and metaphor—a writing style unique to John. Consider the unusual way the writer ends the Easter story. After his resurrection, Jesus appears on the shore of the Sea of Galilee and calls out to Simon and six other disciples who are on the lake fishing. "Have you caught anything?" And the reply comes back, "Nothing!" Jesus then tells them to cast their net on the other side of the boat, and when they do, they catch so many fish that the net might break. When the disciples reach shore with their haul of fish, Jesus has prepared breakfast of bread and fish.

At the end of the first century—when this gospel was written—the church is like a boat, bouncing around on a sea of turmoil, of questions, of doubt, and of fear. You are a follower of Jesus—a fisher of men, and you are wondering how Jewish you can be and still be a Christian. You are wondering how you can follow someone who is dead. You are wondering if it is worth the condemnation of your Jewish friends and family to be a disciple of Jesus. You are wondering what is going to happen to a movement that has no leader, no organization. You are wondering who should be included in this movement. Are we a group unto ourselves, or are we to share Jesus's promises with others?

Peter is the representative disciple as Jesus asks him, "Do you love me?"

"Yes," comes the response.

Jesus comes back, "How much? Do you love me more than these?"

Is Jesus pointing to the boats and the fishing? Is he pointing to the other disciples? We don't know. What we do know is that Jesus is setting the bar for what it means to be a disciple. After asking the question three times, Peter seems to get it. "You know I love you."

"If that's the case," says Jesus, "then feed my sheep."

John's audience now knows what it means to be a disciple— what it's all about, taking care of the least and the lost.

Doing Versus Believing

We have been told that there are millennials—people between the ages of eighteen to forty—who find church or Christianity to be unimportant and irrelevant. When it comes to matters of religion, they call themselves "none-of-the-above," "spiritual but not religious," or "unaffiliated." There are several reasons for this sentiment, but for the most part, would-be believers are more interested in "what do you do" than in "what do you believe"

Truth be known, there are many church-going, Bible-toting baptized Christians who are in the same place. They are either afraid to admit it, or they don't have the will or the energy to do anything about it. Isn't there a place in God's kingdom for honest seekers? If you look carefully at the gospel accounts where Jesus encounters the lame, the least, and the lost—aren't these people the equivalent to the modern day millennials?

I think of Nicodemus—a Pharisee and religious leader. He can recite Torah frontward and backward. Goes to Synagogue every Saturday. Keeps all the feasts and festivals. Keeps Kosher. Here is a man who, by the standards of the day, was a religious man, well respected by his elders and certainly loves God. He is a believer! But here he is, under the cover of darkness, seeking out this man from Galilee, a devout Jew, who speaks to the unclean and the washed out. He touches lepers, he challenges his rabbinical colleagues and dismisses tradition when compassion is called for. He speaks of the kingdom of God as if it were available to everyone, regardless of their beliefs or station in life.

Nicodemus, I believe, is the poster child for the honest seeker. He feels in his heart and in his head that religion—as it was regarded in his day—wasn't enough. Something was missing. So, here he is, seeking that something more, believing that this man can help him with his doubts. Jesus does not scorn Nicodemus for his doubts or for his questions. Instead, Jesus gives Nicodemus what his heart is yearning for—a faith without the religion. "You must be born from above," Jesus tells Nicodemus.

Nicodemus doesn't get it right away. It's a foreign concept—to be born from above. But I would like to think that before their conversation is over, Nicodemus does get it. "Born from above." In other words, a new way of thinking about what really matters to God. Paul said it best, "Be transformed by the renewing of your mind." Faith is as much a head thing as a heart thing because we tend to become what we think. "Whatever is true," says Paul, "whatever is noble, whatever is right, whatever is pure, whatever is lovely, whatever is admirable—if anything is excellent or praiseworthy—think about such things." Renew the mind, and the heart follows. Imagine what could happen if everyone thought that way. When we think like Christ, miracles happen.

Isn't this what we all need? A paradigm shift? Courage to ask the tough questions? A head and heart that finds comfort and satisfaction in the seeking and in the doing? Questions such as "what do you believe?" or "where do you go to church?" or "what denomination do you belong to" are no longer relevant questions. I think that what we do as followers of the Christ trumps what we believe. Or let me put it this way, doing leads to believing—not the other way around.

EASTER FOG

Several years ago, the family did a lot of tent camping. We just bought a new tent and was anxious to try it out. So, on our way to the New Jersey shore, we stopped at a campground near Chambersburg. We found this nice, grassy area near the creek. What a beautiful setting it was! But things soon turned sour when I tried to put the tent up. Upright pole A did not fit into elbow A, and ridgepole R-1 did not fit into Tee-1.

Once the poles were connected to elbows and tees, I had a frame, but leaning toward one side. Since it was almost dark, we decided to put the tent up anyway, pointing as it did to the north. In the middle of the night, it began to rain, and our new tent sprung a leak. Then, all the air went out of my air mattress. Unable to sleep, I got up and went outside, started a fire, and watched the sun come up. As the sun burned off the fog, I could see across the creek and in the field a horse had just given birth to a foal. The mother was still licking the afterbirth off the baby, almost knocking it over with each lick. All the while I was tossing and turning in a damp tent, on a deflated air mattress, new life was taking place across the creek—in the fog.

When I think of the women on their way to Jesus's tomb that first Easter, it might have been something like that. During the night, they likely tossed and turned, knowing that their teacher, their friend had been crucified. Then as the sun rose, burning off the morning fog, they made their way to the tomb with spices and oil to finish preparing Jesus's body for burial. When they arrived, they could see that the stone sealing the tomb had been rolled back, and the tomb was empty.

When you think about it, much of life is lived in a kind of fog. What do we really know about anything? The really tough questions never get answered. It is a rare thing that upright pole A always fits into elbow A. Life can be like someone going into a blind man's house, moving all the furniture around. The world is a Good Friday sort of place with pains and betrayals, crosses and grief, and sometimes a frightening sense of being alone.

One of the messages of Easter, I think, is that beyond the fog that shrouds this life there is something new taking place. We cannot see it from where we stand, of course, because of the fog. But that's what Jesus came to tell us.

ENJOY THE RIDE

I don't know what I would do without my neighbor, Brian. He has been the source of many a sermon. Brian hauls steel for a trucking company. He is on the road a lot, and you would think that when he is home, he would be stretched out on the sofa or relaxing on his deck in his chaise lounge with an iced tea in one hand and a ham and cheese sandwich in the other. But not so. If he is not cutting grass, he is tinkering with his pickup truck that has close to two hundred thousand miles on it. He is changing the oil or replacing a wiper blade or washing and polishing his black and red pride and joy. This pickup gets more attention than Donald Trump. It's a museum piece. He doesn't call it a pickup. He calls it Molly. Brian and Molly have been married for nearly fifteen years. I asked him one day, "Have you ever thought of trading Molly in for a newer model."

His response was, "I don't believe in divorce."

Then there is my red Nissan Rogue. If a car inspection included the inspection of the interior, I would never get a pass. No sticker on the windshield. I truly believe there is something growing underneath my seat. It's not just the smell. Whenever I turn a corner, I hear this kerthump and then a wheezing sound under me. Many times, I have looked under the seat and find nothing. Once a month or so, I vacuum. It's at such moments that I find things that have disappeared—a nail clipper, a coupon from McDonalds for a free quarter-pounder, nickels, dimes, quarters, straws, candy wrappers, cracker crumbs, or something small and rubbery I can't identify.

I want to be like Brian—take better care of my lady. I have tried. It works for a while. The clean interior lasts maybe a week, but then the dirt fairy returns, and I ponder, *How did this happen?* I fret over it sometimes, but at some point, I surrender to it and realize that I am a messy person. I'll never be Brian. I have accepted the fact that the cheeseburger wrapper that fell on the floor will find its way into the trash—eventually. In the meantime, I focus on things that are more important than keeping a clean car. Things like enjoying the ride.

FUNDAMENTALISM

There is a downside—well, more than one downside—to being a pastor/teacher. People might believe what you are saying. Sometimes, when I can't sleep and am desperate for entertainment, I will watch one of those church services broadcast over the inspiration channel. The preacher is selling all kinds of promises from God, if only you buy his book or set of tapes on how to get rich with God. I am thinking, *There are people out there who will believe this crap!* I know this sounds judgmental, but really! Can't God make us rich without the tapes, or is being rich always about money?

The author of 1 John in chapter 3 says, "If we take the testimony of men at face value, how much more should we be assured when God gives testimony through his Son." I take this as a warning—to be careful about accepting every claim that comes down the pike without scrutiny. I don't necessarily accept the testimony of famous people, just because they are famous. Take Tiger Woods, for example, or Jimmy Baker or Lawrence Taylor. I prefer the testimony of knowledge to the testimony of opinion. I might take seriously the testimony of *Consumer's Report*. Newspaper reporters are supposed to find collaborating sources for their stories. The Old Testament even says that no one should be convicted on the testimony of one person. There must be two or three confirming and agreeing testimonies to make things stick, and there is a very good reason for the legal system to reject "hearsay" evidence.

In the early 1900s, there was a knee-jerk reaction to the liberal theology espoused by theologians such as Rudolph Bultmann, Paul Tillich, and Harry Emerson Fosdick. This negative reaction came in the form of a movement called *fundamentalism*. Liberal theology was liberal in the sense that it questioned the assumptions of the Great Awakening in the 1800s, a movement that focused on the emotional side of faith and religion and took the Bible as a literal testimony of what God said as it appeared on the printed page. The liberal theologians made use of homiletical tools such as *form criticism, literary criticism,* and *historical criticism* to get at the context of scriptural passages, to get behind the words and expressions on the printed page, and to find out what Jesus meant, not necessarily what he said. This made a lot of Christians nervous because if the Bible is not true in part, then it cannot be true in whole. And so, the fundamentalists became suspicious of anything scholarly or nonliteral when it comes to interpreting Scripture.

The debate rages on in today's church over whether the Bible is the literal word of God like the Koran, or the truth of God's word expressed in a variety of ways. John Wesley suggested that when it comes to checking our sources, we should make use of a multiple of testimonies—*r*eason, *e*xperience, *s*cripture, and *t*radition. In other words, the Bible comes to life and takes root when brain and heart come together, when faith and reason, religion, and science shake hands rather than sneer at each other and call each other names.

We should never be afraid of the truth—if we are, then we are hiding something—or we are hiding. We are placing a fig leaf over our insecurities. If the Bible is truth, then it will not only withstand the scrutiny of multiple testimonies—it will separate itself from so-called sacred books that have fallen from the sky or were found under a rock—or were the product of someone's wild imagination.

GETTING PAST THE TEARS

Several years ago, there was a man in town who lost his wife when their car stalled on the railroad crossing and was hit by a freight train. He blamed himself for his wife's death because he could have, should have done something to prevent it. After his wife's death, Clyde became a recluse. He was rarely seen in public, and the house was always dark and shades drawn. Then suddenly, he began to show up at funerals. He attended more funerals than the preacher. He, in effect, became a professional mourner. This was his way of working through his grief. By taking the grief of others upon himself, he diminished his own. He was comforted, not in spite of his grief, but *because* of it. It gave new meaning to Jesus words, "Blessed are those who mourn, for they will be comforted."

I know that many of you have wounds that are hidden and deep. I know that you are doing the best you can to overcome the pain of loss, the pain of rejection, the pain of love gone sour, and the pain of disillusionment and disappointment. But it sticks in your gut like gum on the bedpost. *I'll never get past this,* you are thinking. Maybe you feel like Charlie Brown who, one day, was standing with Linus and leaning on the fence with a weary face resting on his hands. They both were consumed with sorrow and depression. Linus says to Charlie Brown, "Sometimes, I feel like life has just passed me by. Do you ever feel that way, Charlie Brown?"

Charlie Brown replies, "No. I feel like it has knocked me down and walked all over me."

Blessed are those who mourn? How can that be? How can it be a good thing to cry? In some Jewish homes there is, on the mantle, what is referred to as a tear cup. It was once a custom that when a tragedy occurred, this cup was held under the eye and the tears collected and the cup placed on the mantle. Archaeologists have found such cups in ancient ruins in Palestine. Of all things, why collect tears? Maybe because tears moisten the soil of healing. It is thought that this is the cup that Jesus was referring to in the Garden when he prayed, "Lord, if it be thy will, let this cup pass from me." The cup in the garden was the cup of tears, and yet it was that very cup that made our salvation possible.

I read an ad in the paper once that read, "Feeling lonely? Hurting? Can't stop crying? Call 796-4237." Out of curiosity, I called the number and the voice on the other end said, "First United Methodist Church. This is Denise." The church of Jesus Christ is in the business of healing. It is in the business of collecting tears, turning brown into green, tears into joy; and we are looking for volunteers.

God Is Fond of Me

In the movie, *Amadeus*, a devout man named Salieri has a deep desire to create an immortal work of praise, but has no aptitude. He is infuriated that God has lavished the greatest gift of musical genius ever known on an impish preadolescent named Wolfgang Amadeus Mozart. In the movie, the question is raised, "Why does God reward undeserving brats?" A line from the play expresses the scandal, "What use, after all, is man if not to teach God his lessons?"

The older I get the more a fan of grace I have become. Maybe it's because I am worn out trying to prove to God that I am worthy of his attention. Maybe it's because I have accumulated too much bitterness toward undeserving brats. Maybe it's because the little house of religion I have built over the years has too many cracks in its foundation, or maybe it's because I have finally realized that getting saved is not the *raison detre* for following Jesus. Whatever the reason, I have decided to take grace seriously and at face value—at great risk I might add—because now it's out of my hands

Brennan Manning tells the story of an Irish priest who, while on a walking tour of a rural parish, sees an old peasant kneeling by the side of the road, praying. Impressed, the priest says to the man, "You must be very close to God." The peasant looks up from his prayers, thinks for a moment, and then smiles, "Yes, he's very fond of me."

What I find intriguing is how hard I have fought against the idea that God is very fond of me, just the way I am. I remember my sister getting ready for her first date—it was a scream. She had bought a new dress that had more lace on it than the Pope's robe.

She bought new shoes. She got a perm. As she stood in front of the mirror, she lamented the fact that she had a long nose and a dimpled chin. Though she did not say it, I surmised it. She was wondering if what she is about to present to her date is acceptable. She didn't realize that her date was already fond of her.

That's the battle we have when we do not accept grace at face value. We will spend most of our lives in front of a mirror, as if preparing for a date with God, asking ourselves if we are an acceptable date. We believe that God will be more pleased with someone who has been cleaned up and washed up and dressed up. Believe me, it's an act of grace on our part when we just show up.

Hand-Me-Down Faith

Some of you can relate to this. I was one of six children in my family—two brothers and three sisters. My father was a plumbing and heating contractor and a workaholic. After all, when you are raising six kids, there is nothing else to do but to work. We were not poor by any means but nothing was wasted. When we had chicken for Sunday dinner, there was the usual drumsticks, white and dark meat. But my dad always prepared a dish of what he called chicken a la gizzards—want not, waste not. This was true of clothing. I inherited my brothers' pants and shirts when he left home, and my younger brother inherited the same clothes when I left home—the same with the girls. This was a hand-me-down family.

As I became active in church as a youth, it occurred to me that most of the sermons I heard were the same every Sunday. They were about sin and what to do about it, how to avoid it, and how it keeps you out of heaven and into hell. Even at the age of twelve, I thought to myself, *This can't be all there is.* And it occurred to me that what people came to believe in was a hand-me-down faith, that is, they came to believe what their parents believed, and their parents came to believe in what their parents believed and so on through the family tree. Inherited faith. In some circles, this kind of faith is called orthodoxy—right belief. One size fits all.

There came a time when I was making enough money that I could buy my own clothes—no more hand-me-downs. And there came a time when I found the courage to question hand-me-down faith and find a place where God wanted me to be. You cannot wear someone else's faith, any more than you can fill someone else's shoes.

We should not disparage the wisdom or our ancestors in the faith. On the other hand, they do not know me as well as God does, and more than anyone else, he knows what fits me and what doesn't.

Happiness Is

I want to tell you something you already know. As fun as Disney World can be, it can't make you happy. A ride and a song can't make you happy. Your spouse can't make you happy. We know instinctively that happiness is not something you catch like a cold. It is not a purchase you make at Sears. You can go to a jeweler and buy a watch, but you can't buy time. You can go to a brothel and buy sex, but you can't buy love. You can pay dues to belong to a club, but you can't buy friendship. You can join the Y and lose thirty pounds, but you can't buy self-esteem.

For the most part, we haven't a clue about what it means to be happy. We have come to associate happiness with possessions, the accumulation of things. I have been watching a TV series called *Hoarders* about individuals who have become obsessed with collecting things, turning their house into a dumpster. You need sonar to find anything—pet feces litter the floor, the smell of decayed animal flesh fills the air. How can anyone live like this? The hoarder generally is mourning the loss of a loved one and unwittingly attempts to replace the loss with clutter—but the clutter only deepens the loss.

I am convinced that it is not happiness we seek, but contentment. The word, "happiness," comes from an Old Norse word, "*hap,*" that means good luck. We get our words, "happen," "happenstance," and "haphazard," from this word. In other words, much of what passes for happiness these days is dictated by our circumstances. Happiness is something that we are always going to find just around the corner or when our ship comes in. "When I get my raise…" "When I get married…" "When I get divorced…" "When I win the lottery…" Such happiness is fleeting and shallow. And when those things *happen*, rather than satisfying our appetite, they only whet it. We have yet to learn the secret that more is less, and less is more.

True happiness is what the Bible calls *joy*. It is serendipitous. It comes through the back door of our lives, not as a reward but as a blessing. Joy is the product of something other than the pursuit of it. It is not something we go after, but something that goes after us. Oddly enough, joy does not come to us as the result of taking something on, but of giving something away. When you make yourself useful to something or to someone, joy comes along in the parentheses.

HEAVEN AND HELL

Heaven and hell—what are we to make of it? Well, I've been thinking. Heaven is sitting on the dock, fishing with your grandson. Hell is not having a grandson—or a dock to fish from. Heaven is being invited to dinner. Hell is knowing that no one will invite you to dinner. Heaven is when a mother holds her newborn son in her arms, still wet and wrinkly from leaving her womb. Hell is a mother holding a baby who will never take a date to the prom because drugs run through her veins. Heaven is sitting on the deck of your house grilling hamburgers. Hell is watching your house float down a flood-swollen river. Heaven is when people look at you. Hell is when people look through you. Heaven is learning that your son is on his way home from Afghanistan. Hell is learning that your son will come home from Afghanistan in a body bag. Heaven is to put your feet up on a recliner, watching reruns of *I love Lucy*. Hell is having no legs. Heaven is blowing out candles on a birthday cake. Hell is watching flames burn down your house. Heaven is the Salvation Army offering a homeless old man a hot meal and overnight lodging. Hell is letting the Salvation Army do all the rescuing. Heaven is finding grace when condemnation is due. Hell is condemnation.

I am convinced that a living hell is much more real than an imagined hell. I am convinced that being forgiven and loved unconditionally is much more real than an imagined heaven. We don't need the promise of heaven and the threat of hell for God to love us when it is already a given. Isn't that why we celebrate Easter?

Hungry For God

I am trying hard to imagine what it means to be hungry and thirsty. I don't know about your refrigerator and freezer, but ours is a warehouse of leftovers. There is a container of sloppy jo mix, some macaroni salad, half-empty jars of mayonnaise, ketchup, and mustard. I was looking for a jar of pickles the other day, and as I was making my way through a maze of milk and orange juice cartons, packages of bologna, Swiss cheese and a sundry of other things, I found a tupper ware conainer of tuna salad that was changing color. I *knew* there was some tuna salad somewhere in there!

In our cupboard—same thing. Cans of soup and vegetables, peanut butter, spaghetti, crackers, and boxes of cereal—many of them bearing expiration dates. There is a veritable grocery store in there! And our son, who used to live with us, would come into the living room and say, "There's nothing to eat!" I can't imagine what it means to be hungry or thirsty. Not really.

There are two versions of the Beatitudes. The longer version is found in Matthew, and the shorter version is found in Luke. Matthew spiritualizes everything, "Blessed are those who hunger and thirst after righteousness," "blessed are the poor in spirit." Luke's version, however, is much more down to earth, "Blessed are those who hunger," "blessed are the poor." What's the difference? One is a blessing for the future—the other is a blessing for the now.

In Luke's version, Jesus talks about a hunger and thirst that is more than a temporary inconvenience, something more than sitting in front of the TV with the remote in one hand and a ham and cheese sandwich in the other. The hunger and thirst Jesus is talking about is the kind that peers over an empty cup. It's the kind where people in remote corners of Africa must walk ten miles and back every day to retrieve drinking water. It's the kind where kids rummage through dumpsters behind restaurants to retrieve food left from the plates of customers who are already overfed. We in America do not know much about the hunger and thirst of desperation. We want for nothing, and that is our undoing. And because we have no want of things, we have no want of God.

So, who is right—Matthew or Luke? The answer to lonliness and despair is not just a refrigerator away. The cure for lonliness is not in our medicine cabinet

HYPOCRITES

I am recalling something that Gandhi said when someone was waiving Christianity in his face, "I love your Christ—it's your Christianity that troubles me." I hope that is the right quote—at least it captures the sentiment. My neighbor has no time for Christians—he tolerates me because I let him borrow my garden tractor. "You won't see me in church. Why should I want to mingle with a bunch of hypocrites!" What have we done—or what have we not done—to deserve such an evaluation? In his book, "When Christians Get It Wrong," Adam Hamilton responds to an interview he had with a twenty-four-year-old man named John who had just returned from Afghanistan as an Army Airborne Ranger. In that interview, John was articulate and respectful, but angry with Christians. This interview prompted Hamilton—pastor of the United Methodist Church of the Resurrection in Leawood, Kansas—to set up a web site inviting young adults to tell him where they believe Christians get it wrong. Wow!

The results revealed that criticisms included one or more of five key themes: 1) The unchristian ways some Christians act, 2) The anti-intellectual, anti-science stance of some Christians, 3) Christianity's view of other world religions, 4) Questions related to the role of God in human suffering, and 5) The way Christians view homosexuality. Hamilton addresses these five issues in his book.

When I read about the bad rap the church is getting these days, I get defensive. "Not all Christians are like that," is what I want to say to the skeptics, when what I am really saying is, "I'm not like that!" While it is true that some Christians can be pretty cocky, arrogant, judgmental, superior, condemning, ignorant, preachy, lofty, hypo-critical, inconsiderate, rude, know-it-all, pushy, legalistic, biblically illiterate, put-offish, inconsistent, lame, insensitive, grand-standing, two-faced, egotistic—I am the exception. Okay, so maybe sometimes I do get a bit self-assured, maybe preachy on occasion. But I'm only human. I'm not perfect, you know!

Now, the John who inspired Hamilton's book says that he is not bothered by the fact that Christians are hypocrites because everyone is a hypocrite. He is not expecting perfection from Christians. What bothers John is that Christians won't admit that they are hypocrites. While it may be true that I don't go around saying to people, "I am a hypocrite," like they do at AA meetings, I think I realize that I am a hypocrite. I just like to keep it to myself.

I Love Spring, But…

Spring has a lot going for it. Flowers like daffodils and crocuses have been hibernating underneath the winter crust. The warm sun and the spring rains wake them up and they poke through the crust, blink their eyes, and make us all smile. The dandelions are not far behind. The trees bud and the sap begins to run. How can you not welcome such a sight? But there is a down side to spring. It's the ants. They too sprout from God knows where. You leave a crumb on the kitchen counter and the word goes out, "Hey, guys, there's a crumb on the Cole's kitchen counter." And suddenly, there's a whole army of ants crawling around.

And then there are the woodchucks. They are looking for a place to settle in, and they find that the crawl space underneath the house suits them just fine. It's not so much that they dig holes to get under the house. It's not so much that they chew on the phone line that runs along the skirting. What is so annoying is that they make babies under the house—just below the bedroom floor. In the middle of the night, you can hear the romance taking place. There is thumping, squealing, and romping. Annoying.

I have tried trapping them with a cage, but the last time I did that, all I got was two cats and a skunk. Friends have suggested a number of other remedies—throw a firecracker down the holes, drop mothballs down the holes, place shards of glass at the entrances, or dump fox urine into the holes. Then there is poison.

I try to find the good even in the bad, but as you likely know, it ain't easy. I suppose ants and woodchucks have a right to this world same as me. I suppose ornery neighbors, arrogant bosses, and tattooed adorned hippies have a right to this world as well. I just wish they would annoy someone else.

If You Cause a Child to Stumble

"If you cause a little child to stumble, then someone should tie an anvil around your neck and throw you into the ocean." How's that for consequences? Or "if your hand causes you to stumble into sin, cut it off." Or "if your eye causes you to stumble into sin, pluck it out." Or "if your foot causes you to stumble into sin, cut it off. Better that you should grope and limp into the kingdom of God than to be thrown whole and healthy into hell." Pretty stiff consequences for stumbling, especially when stumbling is one of the things we are good at.

What is Jesus saying? To begin with, context is everything. What would prompt Jesus to make such outlandish remarks? Mark makes a dramatic turn in chapter eight. Jesus predicts his death and resurrection, so what he says in this chapter is said in the shadow of the cross. The issue is discipleship and whether or not we are up to it. Before you sign on the dotted line, do you know what you are getting yourself into? To be a disciple has serious consequences. Everything you say counts. Your life matters. Your words matter. You have power you do not realize you have, and if you use your power as a disciple to cause someone to stumble—to make them weak, or fearful, or cause them to lose faith—then you would be better off at the bottom of the lake.

As people of God, we are always stumbling—talking one way and acting another. Talking about how precious children are, then treating them as if they are invisible—or worse—treating them as punching bags or sexual objects. Talking about the gifts of God, and then hoarding those gifts while people are rummaging through garbage cans. Talking about God's amazing grace, only to save up our hurts like green stamps in a book—the time she did this to me, the time he did that to me, or the time she said that. A catalog of grieves. We all have one somewhere.

You can be sure that people who know us notice these things. They trip over them, just like we do, and some people will even tell you that is why they don't go to church. They don't see any difference between the people who go to church and the people who don't.

There are days when I wish I had not joined up—I'm just not up to it. I can't stand my own stink. What did I get myself into? Who am I to preach? Disciples need to know that we are under the world's microscope. There are people waiting to ambush us the minute we slip up. What the ambushers don't understand is discipleship is about progress, not perfection. It's about growing and sowing. It's about accepting your failures and trusting that God can use even your failures.

This instruction from Jesus in Mark is a hyperbole—an intentional exaggeration—to make a point. And the point is there is a fine line between going to church and being a disciple.

I'm Sorry

God knows how desperate we are for peace, and at the same time, how elusive it is. "Peace on earth, good will toward mankind." Has a wonderful ring to it, but not very realistic. The rift between the Hatfields and the McCoys continues to be lived out in just about every corner of the world. How long have the Israelis and the Palestinians been at it? Remember the cold war between Russia and the United States? Well, it's just as cold as it always was. The sad thing is that there is a cold war going on between Christian groups. If people of God can't get along, then maybe the sort of peace Jesus talked about doesn't have a chance in—well, you know.

There is a formula for peace, however, that does work. I don't mean to suggest it's an easy formula to carry out, but all good things come with a price tag. The formula is summarized in a song that is popular around New Years, "Let there be peace on earth, and let it begin with me." I would argue that peace, whether world peace or Christian peace or family peace, is only possible when we take the initiative. Someone has to be the hero.

When it comes to resolving conflict between individuals— between nations—someone has to be the one to say, "I'm sorry." When I suggest such a move to a couple heading toward divorce, both will say, "I have nothing to apologize for. I did nothing wrong!" But neither will say, "I'm sorry."

Saying "I'm sorry," is not an admission of guilt. Nor is it a sign of weakness. Actually, it is a sign of strength. "I'm sorry." Maybe you were completely innocent. Maybe you were the victim. Maybe you were the one who was right. But as a victim, you have all the power, because "I'm sorry" neutralizes your opponent's desire to get even. It's the Perp who is powerless.

Jesus instructed his disciples, "Therefore, if you are offering your gift at the altar and there remember that your brother or sister has something against you, leave your gift there in front of the altar. First go and be reconciled to them; then come and offer your gift." The formula for peace: *You* take the initiative. *You* be the one to say, "I'm sorry." Saying, "I'm sorry," is not just a formula for peace with your enemy—it's the formula for peace with God. Saying, "I'm sorry," has eternal implications—it is an act of worship. If an offering is given while you are angry with your brother or sister in Christ, God is not pleased with your offering. Isn't this what Jesus is saying?

Of all the New Year's resolutions that are out there, maybe this one is the most important one of all, "I'm sorry."

In Reach of the Extraordinary

Not long ago, my home church had a centennial celebration—one hundred years of ministry. They invited former pastors and members who had gone into full-time Christian work. Two of these became pastors, and I was one of them. We were both asked to give a testimonial at a dinner in the basement of the church and summarize our ministry. So, I talked about my brief career in the Air Force after graduating, Vietnam, receiving a Commendation Medal, getting married, and accepting an appointment as a student pastor while attending college. I gave a chronology of the churches I served, my doctoral work. All in all, it seemed like I had accomplished a lot, and I was feeling pretty good about it.

After the meal, I sat and talked with my Sunday school teacher, who was now in her nineties. *She would be proud of me*, I thought. But the first thing that came out of her mouth was, "Teddy, you never did pay for the basement window you broke, did you?" In the eyes of some people who know you—who wiped your nose, who read you stories, who bounced you on their knee, who paddled your behind, who watched you grow up—you are forever a child.

This gives us a clue as to why it was that when Jesus began his ministry in his hometown, "He could do no mighty work there." When an insight comes to us from the outside, we can often accept it. But when it comes from within, we are often compelled to reject it because it implies that the rest of us have been shortsighted or somehow spiritually lacking. Jesus's hometown took offense at him because he dared to become more than they expected. He became more than the familiar. He became more than the ordinary. What bothered his hometown was that he became extraordinary. Here is a carpenter's son—why doesn't he act like one! Who does he think he is? And why they have asked the question at all becomes the real story.

We expect the son of a genius to become a genius. We expect the son of a king to become a king. It is no surprise to us when the son of an alcoholic becomes an alcoholic. But it's these blacksmiths, carpenters, and plumbers who measure too far out beyond the ordinary that upset us. Why? Because these carpenter's sons keep saying to us that the extraordinary is in reach of all of us. When the Psalmist says that we were made just a notch lower than the angels—and we act like idiots—who wants it rubbed in our noses?

It Happens on Wednesday
Mornings

It happens on Wednesday mornings. A group of guys get together for breakfast at the church. It's not bacon and eggs—usually it's bagels or sweet bread, a Danish, coffee, and juice. Someone might bring in an egg and potato casserole and try to pass it off as his own creation. But we know better. It's not about the food anyway. It's about conversation. The Men's Breakfast each week (or Men's Book Club as some describe it) consists of ten to twelve guys who manage to get up early enough to say that it's breakfast. They discuss a chapter at a time from a book that the group has selected for reading. I have participated in book clubs before, usually with the area ministerial association. The reading on these occasions is usually associated with cutting edge theology or the product of a big name church leader like Bill Hybels or Lee Strobel. Safe reading. There is something poisonous about theological conversations among clergy that smacks of posturing and saw dust. These discussions often turn into a contest to see who can be more articulate and clever.

But this Wednesday morning clutch is different. For one thing, there is a great deal of respect for individual opinions. There are no dirty looks of disapproval, no posturing, and no condescending remarks. The reading is not always safe—in fact, heresy is tolerated as much as orthodoxy. What is safe about Wednesday morning breakfast is the environment. It is safe to be honest. It is safe to bare the soul. It is safe to be a sinner. It is safe to be dumb. In short, you will find in this group a model for what the church can and should be.

I am tempted to contact President Trump and tell him that I have a model for world peace. Before he goes to China to talk about a reduction in nuclear arms, I would invite him to our Wednesday Morning Men's Breakfast—to pick up some pointers on how to negotiate.

Jesus the Exorcist

Ever notice how Mark begins his gospel? There is no baby in a manger. There are no wise men. No angel visitants. Mark begins his gospel with Jesus as a mature adult, and Mark's first portrait of Jesus is not the Good Shepherd, not Jesus the friend of sinners, and not Jesus the prophet or Savior. Nothing that comforting. Mark's first portrait of Jesus is that of an exorcist. Barely twenty verses into Mark's gospel and Jesus confronts a man possessed with a demon. According to Mark, the demon says to Jesus, "What are you doing here? This is my territory and you are not welcome. I know who you are."

So I am wondering, *Why is our first portrait of Jesus in Mark that of an exorcist?* My mind wants to go to the portrait that adorns practically every Christian church in America—Sallman's portrait of Jesus. Sweet and gentle Jesus, Or the portrait of Jesus cradling a lamb in his arms. Or the Jesus who is surrounded by little children. I just have a hard time with Jesus the exorcist.

I think what disturbs me is the reminder that there are forces in this world over which I have no control. There are forces stronger, bigger, and more intelligent that I. Things I can't do anything about. I am most comfortable in a world where things happen for a reason, where 2+2=4, where my team wins all the time, and when I am on the road all I get are green lights. I want a world where you can work hard and get rewarded for your efforts, where if you follow the rules good things will happen to you, and where people who don't follow the rules are punished. I want a world where everyone likes me, where there are hugs all around. That's the kind of world that makes sense. It's the kind of world I can control.

Mark wants to set the record straight from the get-go. There are powers and principalities out there that don't care whether I wear a clerical collar—in fact they salivate when I do. Mark wants us to know that living clean and following the rules are just as likely to get you into trouble as out of it. So, the question is, if that's the way things really are, then how do you live in a world like that?

There is a clue to be found in Paul's letter to the Galatians, "So let us not grow weary in doing what is right, for we will reap at harvest time, if we do not give up." When Jesus confronted his first demon and the demon told him to leave, Jesus stared it down and in effect claimed the demon's territory. How's that for retaliation? The last thing we do as disciples of Jesus is to concede ground to the demons—whoever and whatever they are. Claiming territory for the kingdom of God in the face of opposition is always a win—sooner or later the payoff comes in ways we never expected.

Jesus Was a Chicken

The gospel of Luke portrays Jesus as one who gathers those who are on the outside looking in—those who are despised and those who do not know what it means to be included. Luke chooses a very interesting example. Jesus is on his way to Jerusalem, which is another way of saying that he is on his way to the cross. Herod had beheaded John the Baptist, and upon hearing about Jesus amid reports that he was John resurrected, Herod was perplexed and curious to the point of wanting to have an audience with Jesus.

A Pharisee—one who considered Jesus a friend—comes to warn Jesus. "Get away from here," he says to Jesus, "for Herod wants to kill you." Jesus tells the Pharisee, "Tell that old fox that nothing will deter me from my work." And then he laments over Jerusalem and its troubled past. But it is his choice of metaphors that is so intriguing. "How often I have desired to gather your children together as a hen gathers her brood under her wings…"

Can we think of Jesus as a chicken? Good shepherd, yes. The way, the truth and the life, yes; The vine, the light of the world, the bread of life. But chicken? The chicken, scuttling about, squawking in awkward efforts to nurture and protect her scattered, squalling, peeping, chicks?

But isn't that what Jesus came to do? To gather under his wings the defenseless and the awkward, the scattered, and the anxious? There is the story told of a grass fire in the barnyard. It burned through the farm, and the animals and birds simply didn't have time to run. When the fire had done its worst, the farmer looked at the damage. There was a mother hen, its wings spread wide, its feathers black and burned. The hen was dead. But when the farmer picked up the dead hen, out scampered half dozen chicks. Just before the fire, she had gathered them under her wings in the face of danger, and she gave her life to save them. Yes, Jesus was a chicken.

Just Shut Up!

I was sitting on the porch last evening after a storm passed through. There was a sweet smell in the air that comes only from a warm summer rain. The darkness seemed different too as if it was hiding something, daring you to pierce through the darkness and discover something you had never seen before. There was a kind of holiness in the quiet of the night. Then, as if someone turned on a light switch, fireflies rose up out of the grass and did their thing. If I allow my head to wander to the biology of fireflies, why they blink the way they do, attracting mates, the magic and the mystery disappeared. I preferred to think that they were putting on a show just for me. They were blinking at me.

It occurred to me that there are things to hear and things to see that come only out of darkness, out of mystery, when our eyes shut down and a different kind of vision takes over. Our brain sees differently as well when there is nothing to stimulate it other than the quiet. I would like to say that it was an out of body experience, but that wouldn't be true—in fact, it was the opposite. In a strange sort of way, my body seemed more real because the experience affected all my senses. I think it is possible to become more real, more grounded, and more in touch when we realize that the greater truths are shrouded in mystery, waiting to be discovered.

We think too much and talk too much—that's what I learned from that porch experience. Our brain is constantly processing our surroundings, categorizing everything, and putting things in order. We like order, and when it comes to communicating with others, we believe that the only way to do that is to talk, get a word in, defend your position, and talk to instead of talk with. We think we are elevating ourselves when we reduce others to objects.

Certainty and order are needed if we are to prevent chaos in our lives. But I would like to put in a word for mystery. Do you know where this word, "mystery," comes from? It comes from a Greek word that means "to close the lips," that is, "to shut up." There are visions and voices that come to us out of the darkness that heal and renew—if we would just shut up!

Koinonea

In the gospel of Luke, everyone is eating. There are a number of banquet stories in Luke. And when Jesus calls Levi to discipleship, Levi responds by inviting Jesus to his house for dinner. Jesus goes to the house of Mary and Martha—and while Mary is having conversation with Jesus, Martha is in the kitchen preparing dinner. There is the parable of the Friend at Midnight. A man rushes to the house of a friend to borrow a loaf of bread, in the middle of the night! In the trilogy of parables—the Lost Sheep, the Lost Coin, and the Prodigal (Lost) Son—they celebrate the recovery of the lost with a party.

There is a line in Luke's companion volume, the Acts of the Apostles, that summarizes the church long before it was defined by creeds and doctrines, "They devoted themselves to the apostles' teaching and fellowship, to the breaking of bread and the prayers." And later, "Day by day; as they spent much time together in the temple, they broke bread at home and ate their food with glad and generous hearts, praising God and having the goodwill of all the people." Eating in Luke is another word for fellowship—*koinonia*.

Koinonia is not just socializing—apes in the rain forests do that. Koinonia is not just sharing information or sharing a common goal—a bowling league does that. What distinguishes koinonia from all other forms of fellowship is sharing Christ. Jesus's promise to his disciples was that anytime two or more of you get together, I will be in your midst. That's koinonia.

A friend of mine said some months after her husband died, "In the depths of my grief when people came to visit, I appreciated the ones with the good casseroles far more than the ones with the bad theologies." Fred Craddock tells about the time he attended a worship service in an old country church in eastern Tennessee. After the service, there was a baptism in a pond behind the church. After the baptism, they all gathered around a fire for food and fellowship. They then formed a circle around the candidate, and one by one, people stepped out and introduced themselves, "Hi, I'm Jordan, and I am a mechanic. If you ever need anything done to your car, call me—no charge. Then an elderly woman stepped out, "I'm a grandmother of ten, and if you ever need a babysitter, call me—no charge." Then another, "My name is Patty, and I bake a lot. Whenever I bake a pie, I'll bake one for you too," and so on.

As the evening and the fire began to wane and people started to leave, Fred stayed behind to help clean up. The custodian walked over to the fire to put it out and said to Craddock. "This is as close to heaven as I'll ever get this side of the grave." Everyone there that evening had something to offer, but it wasn't just conversation. It wasn't just a handshake and a smile. What they offered was koinonia. What they offered was Christ.

LEFT BEHIND

No Child Left Behind: Requires all public schools receiving federal funding to administer a statewide standardized test annually to all students. This means that all students take the same test under the same conditions. Schools that receive Title I funding through the Elementary and Secondary Education Act of 1965 must make Adequate Yearly Progress (AYP) in test scores (e.g., each year, fifth graders must do better on standardized tests than the previous year's fifth graders). If the school's results are repeatedly poor, then steps are taken to improve the school. I like that—children deserve all the breaks we can give them!

No Soldier Left Behind: It's one of the core values of the US military. So, when Private Bowe Bergdahl went missing in 2009 and was believed captured by the Taliban, the Army immediately set about trying to find him. Their efforts cost the lives of six US soldiers. Imagine being wounded in combat—surrounded by enemy forces—knowing that your fellow soldiers are looking for you and will not give up until they find you. I like that.

No One Left Behind is a nonprofit organization that serves families in Orange County, Florida, and surrounding cities. They assist families—particularly children—by offering food, basic staples, and other essentials to live. There are tens of millions of children who are underfed or homeless. They struggle just to survive. NOLB is committed to ensure that no child goes to bed hungry. Like that too!

No Sheep Left Behind: So, he told them this parable, "Which one of you, having a hundred sheep and losing one of them, does not leave the ninety-nine in the wilderness and go after the one that is lost until he finds it? When he has found it, he lays it on his shoulders and rejoices. And when he comes home, he calls together his friends and neighbors, saying to them, 'Rejoice with me, for I have found my sheep that was lost.' Just so, I tell you, there will be more joy in heaven over one sinner who repents than over ninety-nine righteous persons who need no repentance." Awesome!

Left Behind: So, there are agencies and benevolent organizations in our society that exist so that no one should be without or suffer alone. We build hospitals to recover the sick, safe houses for victims of spousal abuse, drug rehabilitation centers to recover those who have turned to controlled substances to deal with their reality, and mental health rehabilitation centers. But according to some Christians, when Christ returns, he will rapture those who are saved and leave the rest behind to suffer the horrors of the Great Tribulation. Don't you find that a bit strange? I'm just asking.

Let Me Tell You About Aunt Evelyn and Uncle Alfred

Let me tell you about Aunt Evelyn and Uncle Alfred. They are like salt and pepper—opposites. If Aunt Evelyn says it's cold outside, Uncle Alfred would say that it's warm. If Aunt Evelyn says the ice tea was too sweet, Uncle Alfred would say it was too tart. Even in religion they couldn't agree. Aunt Evelyn argues that faith is the most important thing. "Prayer is the key to heaven," she was fond of saying, "but faith unlocks the door." And she has the Scriptures on her side. Didn't Jesus say that if you have faith the size of a mustard seed, you can move mountains? But Uncle Alfred has Scripture on his side too. Didn't James say that faith without works is dead? "Without good deeds," says Uncle Alfred, "faith is so much pie in the sky in the sweet by and by." Another of his favorite isms is that people use faith as an excuse for laziness. "God helps those who help themselves!"

Sometimes, I think Aunt Evelyn is right, for there are people in this world who do good deeds but they do not walk with God. But sometimes, I think Uncle Alfred is right, for the world is full of people who are so heavenly minded that they are of no earthly good. So who is right? Is it faith? Or is it works? Is this one of those which-came-first-the-chicken-or-the-egg conundrums? Martin Luther launched the Protestant Reformation on the war cry, *solo fide*—faith alone. Martin Luther King Jr. launched the Civil Rights Movement on the war cry, *I have a dream*. Clearly, it is not faith alone or works alone that lays hold of the power.

There is a middle ground. It is found in the word, "meek." "Blessed are the meek," said Jesus, "for they will inherit the earth." This word, "meek," as it is used by Jesus does not mean that we are to become marshmallows. On the contrary, this same word in Jesus's day was used to describe the way animals are trained to perform certain tasks. It's the same word used for the reigns of a horse. In other words, to be meek is to be in control, to know when to get mad and when to use a soft word, and to know when to speak and when to shut up. To be meek is to know when to act and when to pray.

Isn't that what we need most in our day? We live in a day of extremism and knee-jerk reactions, of suicide bombs along the road to Baghdad and burning crosses in front yards. It's either our way or the highway. It's heaven or hell, you're in or you're out, you're a Christian or a heathen. This kind of either/or theology has given the church a black eye and has caused centuries of bickering, violence, and hate in the name of Jesus. "You start by taking an eye for an eye," said Gandhi, "and pretty soon the whole world is blind." Jesus taught that you overcome hatred and violence, not with brute force but with brute patience. It's the soft word that crushes the stone. The middle ground isn't just compromise or some kind of Platonic moderation. It is giving the love of God a chance to work its way into our skin.

Let's Make Room for Doubters

Imagine having someone in your congregation who knew Jesus. Someone who walked with him, ate with him, and talked to him. What a difference that would make in your faith! It would be like talking to someone who knew Elvis Presley. "You talked with Elvis? You had lunch with Elvis? He gave you his autograph? Wow!" What an advantage the early Christians had! No wonder they had a full crowd on Sunday morning! It was easy to believe back then, and isn't that the problem? We can understand the early church's enthusiasm. We can understand why thousands were converted at one time. Every Sunday Peter or Mary or Thomas would stand up and say, "I saw him, and he's alive!" There are advantages to firsthand faith.

That was two thousand years ago. There are no Peters or Marys of Thomases to give us testimonials and raise goose bumps on our arms. It's sort of like those you-had-to-be-there jokes. It seems to me that the biggest obstacle to resurrection faith is we weren't there. We have to take their word for it. How does the modern Christian live out the resurrection faith secondhand? More importantly, is there room in the church for Christians who say, "I have trouble with this?" Is the church today a safe place for the believer to say, "I know I should be confident about this. I know I should live as if Jesus indeed has risen—but I'm not there yet"? Is there room in the church for this kind of honesty?

If there is no room for such honesty, then what we have are Christians who are living off the faith of someone else. They will give up on their own pursuit of God and simply borrow the faith of those who, like Mary and Peter and Thomas, seem to have it together. I read about a man who, in a moment of confession, told his pastor that he had doubts about the resurrection. "What you need is the faith of your grandmother. Now there was a Christian!" So, he did everything he could to copy her faith. He read her Bible, all dog-eared and underlined, hoping that her faith would leap off the pages, hoping that her marginal notes would light a fire in his heart. He even put on her spectacles as he read, hoping that he would see the same things she saw. But all he saw was blur. One day, while reading her Bible, a piece of paper fell out. He opened the note—a quote from Alfred Lord Tennyson, "There lies more faith in honest doubt, believe me, than in half the creeds."

Frederick Beuchner announced that doubt is the ants in the pants of faith. There is a reason why John decided to include the testimony of Thomas and his doubts. Isn't this the road that Jesus took—the road of doubt and scars? Wasn't there a moment in a quiet garden when Jesus teetered on the edge of uncertainty? Let's hear it for the Thomases. Let's hear it for the epileptic in Mark's gospel who says to Jesus, "Oh, I have belief! Help me with my unbelief!" Let's hear it for those who follow Jesus but pray with their fingers crossed.

Little Things Mean a Lot

If I were to make a New Year's resolution—I'm not saying that I am—but if I did, it would be that I will pay closer attention to the little things. I'm going to take my cue from a group of sixth graders in Iowa who counted the cherries in McDonald's apple pies and found that there were six fewer cherries in the pie than was pictured on the carton. They complained to McDonalds execs, so McDonalds discontinued printing cherries on their cartons. Who would ever think to pay attention to such details?

In chapter 28 of Matthew, Jesus is describing the criteria for entering the kingdom. In the Parable of the Sheep and Goats, Jesus says to the righteous, "You gave me food, you gave me a cup of cold water, you gave me the shirt off your back, you welcomed me, you visited me—and because you did these things, you will inherit the kingdom." And then he says to the self-righteous, "Because you did not do these things, you will be cast into outer darkness!" The self-righteous are condemned because they overlooked the small things. What's a cup of water? What's a shirt? What's a little old visit? What's a welcome? Jesus says, "It's everything!"

We had a poor widow lady in our church who remembers everyone in our family with a birthday card and in that card, there is always a dollar bill. It's just a dollar. You can't eat out on a dollar. You can't buy a gallon of gas with a dollar. What's a dollar? It's a lot because this lady can't afford to give away even a dollar. For some people, little things mean a lot.

We have a man who calls us now and then. He just wants to know how we are doing. Are you over your colds? Do you need anything? It's just a phone call, isn't it? But I can tell you that little things mean a lot.

When Jesus saw the crowd and realized it was near lunchtime, he asked Philip how they were going to feed them all. Where's the nearest McDonalds? Philip responds, "It would take more money than we have to feed this crowd!" Then Andrew chimes in almost apologetically, "Well, there is this kid who brought his lunch with him, but how far would that go?" Five loaves and two fish. It's just a lunch. But Jesus turns it into a banquet for five thousand with food left over. It's not important how he did it, but what is important is what Jesus can do with just a little.

January is usually when the church takes stock of what it needs to do to make ministry happen. There is the budget—will we get enough people to commit to the budget? There is leadership—will enough people step up to the plate to serve on committees? I know that these are real issues to address. But I believe that more important than counting noses and nickels is the little things that will get overlooked because they are seemingly incidental. I'm talking about a cup of cold water—a visit, a kind word, a greeting, a welcome, or a shirt. You know, kingdom stuff.

Living With the Unknown

There are some signs that Easter was here. For one thing, there are a few vases of Easter lilies left that have not been taken home by the donor. And you might notice the faint smell of hyacinths still lingering in some corners of the sanctuary—not to be confused with the smell of cologne or perfume that accompanies Easter dress. I don't know how to negotiate the Sunday after Easter. Neither did the disciples. The book of Acts tells us that just before his ascension, the disciples asked Jesus, "Lord, is this the time you will restore the kingdom of Israel?" And Jesus's answer was not only disappointing to the original disciples, but disappointing to modern disciples as well, "It is not for you to know…"

How do we deal with this "it is not for you to know"?

This answer might have been easier for the disciples to accept if Jesus had left some sort of game plan for them to follow, some clues as to how to organize the church, but he didn't. A mother stands in front of a small casket that contains a baby girl who died of crib death, and her only question is, "Why?" A tsunami hits Japan and thousands are left homeless with the prospect of more tremors. "Why?"

Things would go a lot easier if God would just give us a clue as to why good people suffer and idiots do not, why tornadoes seem to drop right on top of towns and cities rather than dropping harmlessly in the desert, why greedy and greasy handed pimps get away with trafficking young, teen-aged girls, and why in the name of religion we oppress and condemn one another. If God really wanted good things to happen, then why doesn't he shave the odds? I am not impressed with "it's not for you to know…"

So, how do we negotiate this post-Easter dilemma? There may be a clue in what the disciples did. "They went to the room upstairs, where they were staying," and there, they "were constantly devoting themselves to prayer." What I think this means is that by ourselves, we cannot deal with "it's not for you to know" because we have only our disappointments to go by. It takes the collective hope of the faith community to live with the unknown.

Looing at God's Back

Some things in the Bible are just plain weird. In the book of Exodus, while Moses was leading the Hebrews through the wilderness, the people started complaining that they were thirsty. So, God instructs Moses to strike a rock at the foot of Mount Horeb, and when he does, water flows from the rock. The same event is recorded in the book of Numbers, but in this account, God tells Moses to *speak* to the rock, but Moses strikes the rock with his staff instead. Water flows, but because Moses doesn't do exactly as he was told, God tells him that he will not enter the Promised Land. Huh?

But there's more weirdness. While Moses is up on Mount Sinai receiving the Ten Commandments, the Israelites have melted down all the gold earrings and gold cufflinks to fashion a golden calf to worship. While Moses is up there in that rarified atmosphere, God tells Moses about the idolatry going on below and that he is going to consume the lot of them. But Moses is able to change God's mind, and the people are spared.

More weirdness. In Genesis chapter 33, the writer talks about a tent of meeting. This is a tent that was set up just outside the Israelite camp where Moses and God meet up to chat. The people know that God is inside the tent with Moses because after Moses enters the tent a pillar of cloud descends and lands at the entrance. On this particular occasion Moses, wants God to reveal himself. Up to now, God has revealed himself in things like storms, lightning and thunder, glowing clouds—but never directly. "Show me your face," says Moses.

What happens next is not so weird, however. In fact, it makes perfect sense. God instructs Moses to hide in a cave, and when he passes by the cave, he will cover Moses with his hand; and when he removes his hand, Moses will get to see his back, but not his face. The Jews believed that no one can look into the face of God and live. To see God is like looking into the sun—his radiance would blind us.

I believe there is a deep hunger in us all to know God, to meet and greet him. We are told, however, that in spite of our best efforts, God is not knowable in the same way we can know ourselves and others. When it comes to that, we have the advantage of looking at skin, hair, eyes, and ears—things that make us stand out and recognizable. But since God does not have skin, hair, eyes, and ears—we have to rely on something else. God's revelation of himself is always indirect. We know that God has passed by because we have been transformed by his love and grace. We have seen his back.

As disciples of Jesus, we have come to rely on Jesus as the eyes and ears and skin of God. That's why it is so important to come to know who Jesus is—for the more we know about Jesus the more we know about God.

MOSES DILLER

I have this recurring dream that I am the pastor of Riverside Church in New York City—the church of Harry Emerson Fosdick, at one time the most highly prized, the most prestigious pulpit in America. I am preaching with the authority of Billy Graham, the voice of Peter Marshall and the enthusiasm of Billy Sunday, and everyone in the audience in captivated and mesmerized. A multicolored light is beaming its way through the glass stained window over my head, creating this halo over me. I am like Moses, standing on Mt. Sinai, delivering the Ten Commandments—robe flowing and waving like the American flag.

The dream ends with people shouting accolades and applauding. Now, here is the eerie part. I have a similar dream, not on the same night, all the same ingredients are there—glass stained window, flowing robe, the Moses look—except when I begin to preach, I cannot find my sermon notes. Another scenario is that my notes are in front of me, but they are out of order or pages are missing. The Moses look turns into the Phyllis Diller look, and I am a blubbering idiot and people are booing.

I do not know what to make of this since I am not into dream interpretation. I do believe that our dreams open up boxes that we, in our waking state, are afraid to open. As for the beaming Moses dream, I suspect that it reflects my desire to make a good impression, to draw the crowds and put my best foot forward. I want to do it right, get it right, and make a good impression. Let's call it HPS—the Hollywood Pulpit Syndrome. The bumbling Moses dream perhaps reflects that brokenness that I and every preacher bring into the pulpit, a brokenness and a vulnerability that hides beneath the robe and the stole, hiding but not disappearing. Let's call it the SPS—the Stooge Pulpit Syndrome.

Maybe it isn't all that complicated. I am all too aware that heaven and earth converge there at the pulpit or in front of the classroom. Preaching and teaching is both a privilege and a burden. As Paul put it so well, "We have this treasure in earthen vessels." The treasure, of course, is the Word of God as it is interpreted and proclaimed— sometimes with clarity and authority and sometimes with stumbling and groping. Therein lies the rub. How can God trust any of us with such a treasure, weak and trembling and fumbling as we are?

It astounds me that God is willing to take such risks with his Word, whether preaching, teaching, or just doing. And yet Scripture is replete with examples of blundering idiots God used to get things done. David was an adulterer. Moses was a stutterer. Jacob was an arrogant show off. Peter was hot headed and bombastic. Paul, in his own words, was a bigot. And speaking of Paul—he was a perfection-ist! He knew the Hebrew Scriptures forward and backward—a Jew among Jews. But he had an illness, an imperfection he referred to as a "thorn in the flesh." If God would take that away, things would be even more perfect. But God said, "No. Deal with it! Your pain will make you perfect." Maybe that's where you are—looking to be per-fect, but life gets in the way, looking to please God and others, only to discover a gravy stain on your tie.

I guess I should be glad that both dreams are a part of my night-time repertoire. I don't want to be Moses, but neither do I want to be Phyllis Diller. Maybe God is okay with Moses Diller.

Mushrooms and Parsnips

I don't like mushrooms. I don't like them fried with onions. I don't like them on pizza. I don't like them on garden salads or mixed in with spaghetti sauce. I don't like them sautéed, chopped, or stuffed. Don't put mushrooms in my gravy or in my soup. You can cover mushrooms with grated cheese or dice them until they almost disappear, but they are still mushrooms. I don't know—maybe it's because I don't like anything that grows in the dark. Or maybe it's their color—they look like slugs! They are slimy and rubbery. They don't look edible. They are, after all, fungi—relatives of the toadstools and tree rot.

I know people who eat mushrooms. I know people who love them. I still get along with these people, though I think they are strange. On occasion, they try to convince me that mushrooms are good for you, that if you fry them up in butter along with some garlic and lemon juice, they can be quite tasty. They are convinced that if I just try some, I'll learn to like them. I don't think so.

I know what I like and don't like, and once I make up my mind, there's no changing it. After all, I have a right to dislike mushrooms. I have a right to tell others that I don't like them, and I don't like people telling me I am wrong for refusing to put mushrooms over my steak. I like parsnips. I like to roll them in flower and breadcrumbs, dip them in beaten eggs, and fry them up with some onions. People tell me that parsnips are tasteless, and you can't do much with them except boil them until they become paste. But I don't go around making people feel guilty because they won't try parsnips. I am not that hard up for affirmation. They are entitled to their opinion—as long as it's the same as mine.

Q

It is thought by many scholars that the Sermon on the Mount came from the Sayings Q Document, a hypothetical yet very plausible gospel created by the earliest Christian community. It is thought that Matthew and Luke had access to this gospel and that both gospels contain material from Q. In essence, Q was the basis for an alternative community with Jesus' teachings providing the blueprint. When we closely examine the material in the Sermon on the Mount we discover that the fundamental building blocks for this alternative community have to do with relationships—how to get along with your neighbor, how to get along with your spouse, how to get along with those who disagree with you, who lash out at you, how to get along with your enemy. Basic to the health and prosperity of any civilization, let alone a community, is getting along—to live in peace with one another.

The key to any healthy relationship, especially within the alternative community we call the church, is familiarity and proximity. You know what is required for a person to criticize or judge someone else? Distance. There is a distance required to criticize or dehumanize another person. They have to remain strangers. As long as we keep our distance from someone, we can make of them whatever we want. And for many people, it is important to have an enemy or two among their list of acquaintances. Otherwise, they wouldn't know what to do with their prejudices.

Road Less Traveled

M. Scott Peck begins his best seller, *The Road Less Traveled*, with this line, "Life is difficult." No kidding! "This is a great truth because once we truly see this truth, we transcend it." I see another reason why it is a great truth. It says something about what we already know but don't want to know, that life does not come to us ready-made, all mapped out, filleted and ready to serve. Peck points out a common complaint among us humans that our problems, our frustrations, and our tragedies represent a unique kind of affliction that should not be visited upon us.

Like many Christians, I turned to the Bible for answers to life's tough questions, to discover solutions to life's dead ends. But what I have discovered over time is that God is not a helicopter parent, nor does the Bible hand out solutions for every conceivable conundrum. Rather, the Bible speaks to life as it really is—difficult. That life is not an asphalted road with signs to guide us and warn us. The Bible tells us that at best, life is a footpath with an occasional bent twig or over-turned stone to remind us that someone else has traveled this road. The Bible reminds us that before us, there were people like Abraham and Sarah who could not have children. There were brothers like Cain and Abel who could not get along with one another.

There was Naaman who was born a leper. There was a woman Jesus met at the town well who had been alienated because she, in effect, was a woman of the street. There was Peter whose best friend was Jesus. But when Jesus was arrested, Peter denied that he ever knew him. The Bible does not give advice on how to avoid difficulties. What it does do is show us how to own up to them, to deal with them head on.

There is one other truth the Bible offers. Every year, our Jewish friends celebrate the Feast of Sukkot, celebrating the time of wandering in the wilderness. Now, why would they celebrate something like that? What happened in the desert was not something you would want to commemorate. The Hebrews were hungry, thirsty, and boiling under the hot sun by day and freezing under the nighttime sky. They wandered, not knowing where they were going or why. Forty years of wandering. That's something to be forgotten, not remembered! But today, the Jews, not only remember that event, but celebrate it. Why? Because while they were in the wilderness, they became a nation. In the wilderness, they received the Ten Commandments.

In the wilderness, they received the plans for the Ark of the Covenant. In the wilderness, they exchanged their image of a beaten, oppressed people for an image of self-confidence and self-identity. They also learned something about their God—that God is not a helicopter God. They learned that God's best chance at teaching us anything about life is when we have to struggle for it, sacrifice for it, and lean into the wind.

If you look at a map of the Exodus, you will notice that the Promised Land—Palestine—is only about two hundred miles east of the Red Sea as the crow flies. It would take, maybe two months, to get to where they were going. Instead, God took them the long way around by way of the desert. Instead of two months, it took God's people forty years to get home. This is the way of God. If we allow it, God will teach us how to address life, not by taking us the shortest distance but taking us the long way around. In Edward Albee's play, *The Zoo Story*, a character describes life this way, "What I am going to tell you has something to do with how sometimes it is necessary to go a long distance out of the way in order to come back a short distance correctly." When it comes to dealing with struggle and challenge, the shortest distance between two points is not a straight line but a crooked one.

So, What Else Is New?

Cynicism is everywhere—it's even in the Bible. The most famous cynic in the Bible is the author of Ecclesiastes. From beginning to end, the book focuses on one theme: "There's nothing new under the sun." All our efforts are futile. We think we have made some progress, but in the end, it is wasted effort because nothing lasts. We waken in the morning, put our legs into the pants, shave, comb the hair, read the morning paper, and then off to work. At day's end, you return home, pet the dog, eat supper, watch some TV, and go to bed. Tomorrow, the same routine is repeated—over and over again. "What has been will continue to be." This sentiment is expressed on the face of a tombstone:

> While we live, let's live in clover,
> For when we're dead we're dead all over.

You've heard of the law of conservation of energy? The law states that nothing is either created or destroyed. The paper you read every morning gets tossed in the wastebasket and then placed in the burn barrel outside and set afire. That newspaper turns into smoke, moisture, or ash, rises and joins a cloud—but the paper is not destroyed. So, last week's newspapers are floating around up there in the stratosphere, today part of a cloud, tomorrow part of a rain drop—and someday the New York Times will pop up out of the ground in a kernel of corn. Just think—the breath George Washington expelled is still around—maybe you breathed the breath of Washington!

Koheleth chooses an interesting word to describe his cynicism, "All is vanity!" The Hebrew word is "mist." Like mist, our search for happiness and meaning is futile because nothing lasts. It comes and it goes. Round and round—like hamsters in a cage—we circle and we expend energy but get nowhere. How does one counter such cynicism?

At the end of the book, the author has come full circle. He begins as the consummate cynic and ends as the consummate optimist. "Now all has been heard; here is the conclusion of the matter: Fear (respect) God and keep his commandments." It's true that cynicism is rampant in our day. It's all around us, and it's becoming more and more popular. But somehow, in God's own time and in God's own way, everything will have to do business with God.

> This is my Father's word,
> O let me ne're forget;
> That though the wrong seems oft so strong,
> God is the ruler yet.

Special Because We Are Chosen

One of my earliest disillusionments spiritually was when I was about ten or eleven. Along with four other youth, I was going to be baptized. When it came time for the baptism, the pastor noticed that no one had put water in the baptismal basin. He said, "Woops! There's no water. I'll be right back."

He left momentarily to go out to the bathroom to draw some water from the tap. He came back and proceeded with the baptism. I was horrified! I didn't want to be baptized with tap water! City water! Water that had come through a pipeline under the city streets next to the sewer lines! Drawn just inches away from the commode! Isn't baptismal water supposed to be holy water? I never gave much thought to where baptismal water comes from—maybe it was shipped in from the Holy Land, water taken from the Jordan. Or maybe the pastor had the bishop come in and pray over it. I didn't know. I was worried that the baptism wouldn't take hold. I knew that the Catholics used holy water. Why couldn't we borrow some from the Catholics!

Funny how we think about things when we are young, when our brains are still developing—and our faith. I know now that the word, "holy," means "to set apart." What makes something holy is not that it has special properties, but because it is set apart for a special purpose. Even spit can be holy—ask the blind man that Jesus healed. God can take something as mundane and ordinary as tap water and make it special. God can take me—warts and all—and do something with me. God specializes in turning brown into green. So, God calls his people "holy," not because we are deserving or saintly, but because we have been set apart for a special purpose. We are not chosen because we are special, but we are special because we have been chosen. But we so often get it wrong. We get ordained or are selected to teach a Sunday school class or serve on a committee and we think, *I'm special!* or *God likes me because I have a hefty bank account!* or *I'm successful because I am good.* And of course, the converse becomes true, "My neighbor's marriage is falling apart—God doesn't like him." "Those people at the end of the block living in squalor—they must not believe in Jesus."

But that kind of thinking isn't biblical, is it? What did Jesus say, "God makes the sun to shine on the good and the evil; he makes it rain upon the just and the unjust." I take that to mean that my goodness will not prevent my roof from leaking.

I hear people talk about their conversion as if they are doing God a favor. I hear them talk about salvation as if to say, "Whew! I'm in!" But to be saved—to be holy—is not to be saved *from* something but to be saved *for* something. Those people at the end of the block who live in squalor—maybe they would have a chance to be holy too if we would just knock on their door and hand them a fresh baked apple pie.

TAKING KIDS SERIOUSLY

In Mark chapter 9, Jesus conducts a final exam on Discipleship 101. It's a one-question exam, "Who do men say that I am?" Their answers range from "you are Elijah" to "you are the Christ." But Jesus is not satisfied with these answers, so he asks the disciples to review their notes—how he told them that the Son of Man must suffer and die. Don't you remember, John? Don't you remember, Andrew? But Peter still doesn't get it because he tells Jesus that he is wrong. The teacher doesn't know what he is talking about. Messiahs don't suffer and die—Messiahs invade and conquer. But it was Peter who got it wrong—Peter wearing the tank top, showing off his tattoo-riddled arms, strutting around with an attitude and spewing snuff spit. If you got into an alley fight, would you want Jesus to back you up? Hardly.

So, what's all this hype about turning the other cheek, being last in order to be first, losing yourself in order to be found? Does this kind of advice work in a society that shoots first and asks questions later? Jesus and the Twelve have been on the road, and when they arrive in Capernaum, Jesus asks them what they were arguing about back there. The Disciples are reluctant to discuss it because they know they are about to get a lecture. They were arguing about the pecking order in their group—who was the greatest. Why this issue is so important for Jesus is reflected in the fact that his earthly ministry is just about over, and the Disciples still don't get it. It's almost as if everything Jesus tried to teach them hangs on this one truth—if you want to be first, you must be last. If you want to be served, you must be a servant.

To make his point, Jesus chooses an unlikely example. In Jesus's day, children were fillers, not main events. While other people tended to ignore anyone shorter than their kneecaps, Jesus saw what was really going on. He saw the little ones hanging on to their mothers' skirts, sometimes being yanked along. Children were nonpersons, fuzzy caterpillars to be fed and sheltered until they turn into butterflies. So Jesus would take babies into his arms and he would bless them. He knew how to put his hands behind their wobbly heads. He never asked parents to please take their children to the nursery because they were too noisy. "The kingdom of God belongs to such as these," he said. They are full-fledged citizens of God's house—not later, but now.

Do you want to spend some time with God? Then get down on the floor with your little Sarah over there. Get finger paint all over your clothes, laugh at her dumb jokes, and never mind that you have an appointment. She is the main event. If you have been having trouble talking to God lately, then go talk to a kid—get used to the language, look at the innocent face, and giggle a little—then you will know how to talk to God.

TALKING RELIGION

I was sitting on the back porch doing crosswords when these two middle-aged ladies walked up. One of the young women was holding the hand of a pretty little blond girl with ringlets—kinda Shirley Temple-ish. I knew instantly that they were Jehovah's Witnesses come to visit. They were pale-looking, wore ankle-length dresses, and had a Bible in their hand. "Beautiful day, isn't it?" said the woman holding onto the cute little girl's hand. I agreed. She did not introduce herself, her companion, or the little girl. "I wonder if we could take a few minutes of your time to talk about the promises of God?"

A part of me wanted to tell them that Donna had just called me in for supper, but I invited them up on the porch. "The Scriptures are full of unfulfilled prophesies that are even now beginning to unfold," said the talkative one.

I interrupted, "Did you tell me your name?"

"Oh, my name is Candice, and this is my daughter, Patricia, and this is my friend, Janice. Now, if you look in the book of Daniel, you will find a map for the future."

I interrupted once again. "Patricia, how old are you?"

She slid behind her mother and did not answer. Candice opened up her Bible. "Daniel prophesies the birth of Christ. If you look in Daniel chapter nine…"

"So, Janice, are you from around here?"

Janice wasn't sure what to do or say since her role was to be seen and not heard. "Yes, I live in Erie."

"And you are a Jehovah's Witness?"

She looked over toward her partner as if to ask permission to speak but permission was not given.

"Yes," she answered."

Candice by now was clearly unnerved—this was not going as planned. "If you turn to Daniel…"

I was on a roll. "Janice, do you have children?"

"Yes, I have three."

"And what are their ages?"

"Twelve, nine, and seven."

"I have a daughter who is a dental assistant and a son who still lives at home," I said, "but he will soon be leaving the nest to get married."

"You must be excited," she said. "You are about to gain another daughter."

I said, "Yep. God is good—she is the perfect girl for our son. She knows how to cook and everything."

Janice laughed and I laughed. Candice interrupts, "Getting back to Daniel—"

Janice continued, "My husband is on the police force in Erie."

"High stress job," I said.

"Yes, I worry a lot, but I know he is doing something important."

By now, little Patricia had moved away from her mother and said, "I cut my finger," and she proudly showed me her scar. So much for Daniel. It took some doing, but we finally got around to talking religion.

THAT'S WHY I CAME

Donna and I had a horrendous week. I had a couple of funerals, one of them a suicide. The couple across the road was going through a divorce, and the husband had been calling me all hours of the day and night, sobbing. He couldn't understand why his wife was leaving him just because she saw him kissing the checkout girl at Giant Eagle. So, all that week, I would sneak in and out of the house to avoid the sobber. When I came home at night, I turned the lights out on the car so he wouldn't see me pulling into the driveway. After church, Donna and I decided we needed to get out of town for awhile, so we packed the car and went to a campground for the night. We had just finished pitching the tent. I had made a cozy fire and was sinking into the lawn chair to take in the beauty of nature when who should pull in but the sobber. Somehow, he had found out where we were, and as he got out of his car, he said, "I thought you might like some company."

Mark, the Gospel writer, tells us about Jesus early ministry, how popular he was. He was performing exorcisms and healing the sick. Why wouldn't you want to meet this guy? Mark sums it all up by saying, "At once his fame began to spread throughout the surrounding region of Galilee." Everywhere he went, Jesus had to contend with the crowds. But Mark often uses phrases like, "And he went away to a solitary place for the crowd." "He slipped away, for the crowd was pressing in upon him." He even tells those whom he has healed not to tell anyone. In Mark, Jesus is with the crowds, but he is always avoiding the crowds at the same time. "Don't tell anyone." "Keep it quiet." He even tells the demons to shut up.

Doesn't it strike you funny that Jesus wanted both to be with crowds and avoid them? Crowds are usually an indication that things are going well. I can't think of any institution that doesn't want a crowd. Hospitals want crowds. Football games want crowds. Concerts want crowds. Churches want crowds. There isn't a preacher I can think of who doesn't want a crowd. In this world, a crowd means you are a success. But in the Gospels, crowds are not a sign of success but a sign of fickleness. "The city gathered around the door" in Mark is there to use Jesus, not to follow him. In Mark, the crowd who will one day sing "Hosannas" to Jesus, the next day will shout, "Crucify him!"

One day, Jesus took off and Simon went looking for him. He finds him somewhere in the woods—a campground somewhere—and says to Jesus, "The whole country is looking for you." But Jesus would not go back. "Let us go to the neighboring towns, so that I may proclaim the message there also; for that is what I came out to do." I hope you get it, Simon. People will come from miles to see a healer, but they wouldn't cross the street to listen to a prophet.

The Albino Pig

I understand that some misfortunes come our way through no fault of our own. We are victims. On the other hand, I have noticed how often we want to point the finger in the other direction. When I was growing up, we had a farmer down the road who raised pigs. Once in a while, I would go down there and watch them feed the pigs, watch them dump this stuff into the trough that looked like oatmeal with corn in it. I asked Randy, their twelve-year-old, what they were feeding them, and he said, "You don't want to know." They didn't raise pigs for pets but for butchering. I watched them butcher a pig once, and I threw up.

One day, Randy called on the phone and said, "You gotta see this! Our sow just had a litter of pigs and one of them is an albino. I'll show him to you, but it will cost you a quarter." I never saw an albino pig before, never saw anything albino before. I figured a quarter was worth it.

So, I went down to see, and Randy had the pig in a box, and when I and two other kids forked over our quarters, he opened the box and out ran this albino piglet. He grunted, squealed, and ran around the barnyard a few times when Randy got hold of him and put him back in the box. "It will cost you another quarter if you want to see him again!"

Well, the albino grew and was looking more and more like a pig. He turned out to be a nasty pig. Even Randy didn't trust him. One time, the albino bit him in the leg when he was feeding him. Another time, he smashed his way through the chicken wire fence, killed one of the chickens, and ran off. Randy's dad came down to the house to tell us that he was organizing a search party and would we join in on the search. So, my dad and I went out traipsing through the woods and the swamps, but we never did find him. For all we know, the pig died out there in the woods somewhere from not getting enough slop, and the turkey buzzards feasted on its carcass. Or some family in the next county saw it and made a pet out of it.

There were reports that the albino had been spotted here and there. Ralph, our neighbor, said he was driving home from work around midnight, and the albino ran across the road in front of his truck and disappeared into the brush. "How do you know it was the albino?" my dad asked.

"I know a pig when I see one—besides, it was white."

And there were other reports. People's garbage cans were being ransacked—it must have been the albino. Jeffrey, our neighbor's seven year-old, came running into the house one evening about sundown, screaming that the albino was chasing him. News gets around. A man in Union City said the albino attacked his dog. "Did you see it happen?"

"Well, no, but people around here have seen the albino going through their trash—it had to have been the albino!"

And so it went. As each story got told, the albino got more albino and more ferocious and more dangerous. The way some tell it the albino was six feet tall and had horns, and how did they know it was the albino that they saw? Because it was.

I know it is easy to refer to the imagination when you can't explain something rationally. So, I think the pig got blamed for a lot of trouble it wasn't responsible for.

I often think about the albino when I think about the devil and how it has captured our imagination, how the devil is behind our evil deeds, and how the devil is going around, tipping over our lives and getting us into trouble. I don't know, evil is real, all right. But what if evil is more a product of our own greed than the work of some malevolent deity? What if people are starving and homeless because some whacky dictator decides he wants it all? John from Patmos and Revelation puts the blame where it belonged—on idolatrous Rome.

It's about time that even good people accept responsibility for their own screwups rather than blame the devil—or the albino. What was it that Pogo said, "I have met the enemy—and it is us."

The Church that Became a Deli

When I was in my third appointment, I was sent to a parish of three country churches. Getting around Sunday morning to preach was a Houdini act. This past summer, I drove by one of those churches, and to my surprise, the church had closed and the building turned into a deli and pizza shop. In place of the cross on the front of the building there was a neon sign that flashed "pizza." I stopped to see if I could recover any memories amid the smell of garlic and pizza sauce. In place of the pews were booths. Where the altar rail once stood, there was a counter with a cash register on it. Where the pulpit once stood was a pizza oven, and the choir loft was now taken over by a large walk-in freezer and a table stacked with pizza boxes. I sat down in one of the booths, just to give my brain a chance to make the transition from pulpit to pizza.

I thought about the weddings and baptisms performed there where the counter stood, the folks who came to the altar to pray and give their life to Christ. I thought of the times I broke the bread and poured the cup for communion, just about where they were tossing dough in the air. And above the altar—I mean, counter—were neon menus, displaying pizza and sub options. What did they do with the pulpit? What did they do with the altar? Just then, I noticed that the stained glass windows were still in place. It all seemed so surreal—a kind of oxymoron. Stained glass windows—casting a sacred light into the room, landing on fresh-baked pizza, topped with sausage, cheese, and pepperoni.

And I thought about how Jesus entered the temple one day, saw the money changers conducting business. Is selling pizzas equivalent to selling doves? The booths in the pizza shop—are they equivalent to the tables Jesus turned over?

While I was musing over all of this, a waitress stopped to ask if I wanted to order anything. I ordered a Coke and asked about the church—I mean the pizza shop. How did it come to pass that the church was sold and turned into a deli? She said that when the church decided to close its doors, a number of people were interested in buying the building. One person wanted to turn it into a garage, another a bar, and another a spa. The pizza shop won out. The waitress said, "I think God would be pleased that we are serving pizza rather than booze."

I left, and as I drove away, I looked in the rear view mirror, framing the church turned deli. And I chuckled. Maybe God is pleased—after all, church was going on. People were eating and laughing. Not a bad image for worship.

THE DECORATED JESUS

In a little Roman Catholic Church in southern Bavaria, there is an ornately decorated flute on display under glass. It takes a wild imagination, but tradition has it that this flute belonged to the psalmist, David. It was discovered among some ruins near Jerusalem. Scholars and archaeologists flocked from all around the world to examine this prize find. There was skepticism that the owner of the flute was David, but the find caused so much hysteria that consensus won the day—it was David's flute.

A well-known musician was invited to play the flute, and the sound that it produced was beyond description. Its sweet tones seemed to soothe both mind and body. It was David's flute alight! The flute went on display for all to see. It became a pilgrimage site. Eventually, it was given over to the church as a religious relic. It became an object of worship and reverence.

At first, it was displayed in its original simplicity, in a glass case that was air-conditioned to prevent it from any further deterioration. But as more and more people came to visit, the church decided it was too plain to be revered—so gold leaf was added to the flute. Then it was gilded with gems of all kinds. Soon, the instrument was almost unrecognizable.

One day, the Pope came to visit the lowly church. Preparations were made to receive the pontiff by laying out the red carpet. A concert was planned, an afternoon of sacred music especially arranged for the pontiff, and the featured instrument would be the magic flute of David.

The time came for the concert. All eyes and ears were riveted on the flautist as he brought the instrument to his lips. But alas, the sound that came out was horrifying. The instrument was so heavy and cumbersome from all the ornamentation that it was no longer a flute. Nonetheless, people continued to make a pilgrimage to pay homage to the flute. It could be worshipped, but it was no longer a flute.

The early church had a core message from the get-go. It came to be referred to as *kerygma,* a Greek word that means "proclamation." The core message was this—Jesus is the fulfillment of Scripture. Jesus was born to a peasant family. He was raised a Jew and barmitzvahed at the age of twelve. He was trained as a rabbi and went out into the countryside to proclaim the kingdom of God. He was arrested, tried, crucified, and rose from the dead. Plain and simple. But over the centuries—like David's flute—Jesus has been gilded with creeds and doctrines, displayed on glass stained windows, and has become an object of worship. What have we done to Jesus? Today, he is hardly recognizable.

The Mizpah Blessing

Jacob is on the run, having deceived his father, Isaac, into giving him his birthright rather than to the elder son Esau. He makes his way to a town called Haran, where he falls in love with a woman named Rachel. He strikes a deal with Rachel's father, Laban, and they agree that if Jacob is a good boy, works hard in the family business, and proves his worth as a son-in-law, he may have Rachel as his bride. The catch is, however, that he must first work the farm for seven years.

But Laban is a sly old fox. At the end of seven years, the wedding is held, and this time, Jacob is the one who is deceived. Maybe it was too much wine, or maybe the veil over his bride was extra thick, but after the vows are said, and the ink is barely dry on the marriage license, Jacob realizes that Laban has substituted one of his other daughters for Rachel. He has married her sister, Leah, instead.

Hopping mad, Jacob goes to Laban to ask for a refund. Instead, another deal is struck. Jacob will work for yet another seven years and in exchange Jacob may have both sisters in marriage. Seven more years pass but by now, Jacob is sick and tired of Laban's underhandedness, so he packs the mules, and along with twelve children and his two wives, Jacob makes a run for it. But before they leave, Rachel steals some family heirlooms from Laban, mostly out of spite. Well, the whole thing comes to a head at a little jerk-water town called Galeed or Mizpah. In the meantime—are you still with me—Laban goes off in search of Jacob, believing that Jacob has stolen the heirlooms. When he catches up with the party at Mizpah he accuses, Jacob of theft—not knowing that Rachel is the culprit. Jacob invites

Laban to search the mules, the tents, and promises to kill anyone in the family who has committed the theft.

So, Laban searches high and low. He enters Rachel's tent, turns over the pots and pans, looks through her bags, except the one she is sitting on, which contains the jewels. Laban will not look through this one because Rachel is in the middle of her period. Finding nothing, Laban leaves. Laban and Jacob must come to some sort of terms. Neither is willing to submit. They must make peace or kill each other. So, what do they do? They gather some stones and make a memorial, and over the rocks, they agree to disagree with what has come to be known as the *Mizpah Blessing*, "May the Lord watch between you and me while we are absent one from the other." It is barely a blessing, but it is a blessing because they both have agreed to an imperfect peace, to separate and trust God to take care of the rest.

The *Mizphah Blessing* has come to be a nice way to end a meeting, but in its original context, it was meant to keep enemies from hurting each other. I have many friends who have been wounded and wronged by others, who cannot complete the task of forgiveness—it is too painful. There is something to learn from this ancient soap opera out of the book of Genesis. When perfect peace is not forthcoming—like it or not—we must settle for an imperfect peace. The fact is that not every conflict we have with others gets resolved this side of heaven. That happens only in fairy tales. Sometimes, we have to move on or die inside, move on, and let God sort out the details.

THE PLACE TO BE

On Sunday, July 17, 1966, arguably the most noteworthy worship service was held in St. Peter's Cathedral in Geneva. A great congregation had gathered, including Christian leaders from all over the globe. Reporters from around the world were present to cover the event. The service had been planned as part of the World Council of Churches Conference on Church and Society, and there was an exceptional air of expectation that day since the sermon for the morning was to be delivered by Dr. Martin Luther King Jr.

But Dr. King did not show up. They hymns were sung, the prayers were prayed, and the ecumenical affirmations were spoken, but the pulpit was empty. Dr. King had canceled his trip to Geneva at the last minute because of racial rioting in the city of Chicago, and his presence was needed there to mediate the crisis. He sent a videotape of an excellent sermon to the Geneva conference, and it was played over television monitors at the appropriate time, but as one worshipper pointed out, "Even more powerful than his sermon that day was Dr. King's absence."

If Dr. King had been a politician, raising campaign funds, he would have been there. If Dr. King had been looking for a photo op, he would have been there. What appeared on the surface to be the most important place for him to be turned out to be the second most important place for him to be.

THE PROBLEM OF THEODICY

For centuries, scholars and theologians have struggled with the problem of theodicy. Theodicy comes from two Greek words put together—*Theo* or God and *dici* or justice—the justice of God. The problem of theodicy, in other words, deals with the justice of God, or as some would put it, the injustice of God. The debate goes something like this:

> If God is all-powerful and able to prevent suffering but is not willing, he is malevolent.
> If God is all loving and willing to prevent suffering but is not able, he is impotent.
> If God is both all-powerful and loving, then why is there suffering?

Why does God allow some people to suffer while others seem to escape it? C.S. Lewis notes that theodicy is atheism's most potent weapon.

And I can understand that. Why would a loving and caring God want anyone to suffer? My faith is most at risk when I am hurting or when I witness pain and suffering in others. And why is that? Because faith is so often associated with prosperity. Faith that does not produce positive results does not make sense. Why ride a bus that doesn't take you to the amusement park? Or to the supermarket? Or to the ball game? In other words, in my mind, I can believe in God as long as I get what I want and as long as my faith takes me to where I want to go. It's the way I am wired. I can't help it. I am consumer oriented. Everything from my checkbook to my relationship with others is geared to satisfy my need to be happy, prosperous, and healthy.

To be a person of faith requires an attitude adjustment. Not everything is about me. Not everyone is obligated to make me happy—including God. I am entitled to nothing. God is not a cosmic Santa Claus who is making a list and checking it twice and acts depending on whether we are naughty or nice. As for pain and suffering, it comes with the human condition. Health and prosperity are not evidence of God's existence any more than pain and suffering are evidence of his absence.

Fred Craddock met a man who was born with no arms. He said his mother fed him and dressed him until one day she put his clothes in the middle of the room and said, "Here, dress yourself." And she left the room. He kicked and screamed, "You don't love me anymore," he kept screaming. Finally, realizing that his mother was not going to dress him, he began manipulating his toes, picking up each article of clothing until finally he dressed himself. "It wasn't until later that I knew my mother was in the next room crying." Sometimes, love is like that.

THE RADICAL CENTER

According to the Pew Institute, nearly 40 percent of the American population under the age of forty are religiously uncommitted. These are young adults who purposely avoid church membership, and when asked if they belong to a particular church or denomination, they use words like *unaffiliated, non-denominational, marginally Christian, spiritual but not religious* or *other.* Around 26 percent of the population say they belong to a particular church or denomination and participate in organized and traditional forms of religion. Is there a message here?

If, in fact, this describes American Christians, then church as it was fifty years ago until now does not reach those who consider themselves interested in Christ but not in organized religion. Studies show that this population of "spiritual but not religious" is interested in orthopraxy (right practice) over orthodoxy (right belief).

In my mind, the challenge for the modern church is to find that "sweet spot" that Wesley referred to as the *radical center,* a place where you belong to Christ, not to a denomination. Wesley was concerned that the established church of England was ignoring the plight of the poor, the outcast, and the dregs of society. As an Anglican priest, Wesley tried to move the church in a more inclusive direction, but the established church resisted. So Wesley took the church to the streets, the ghettos, the coalmines, and the fields. He organized societies—small groups—that met in homes to study Scripture and hold one another accountable.

The established church refused to give Wesley a pulpit as long as he was "improperly delivering the gospel." But that didn't matter to Wesley. He continued to establish societies all over England, and Methodism grew and spread to the colonies in the new America. So, Methodism has *inclusiveness* in its genes and the desire to remove labels that exclude, judge, and condemn. Is it time, once again, to take the gospel to the streets? Is it time, once again, to welcome the tattooed, the rejected, the dirty, the trailer trash, and the indignant? Can we welcome sinners, even if they do not qualify as religious? I hope so.

There Is No Church Like That

Tony Campolo tells about being invited to speak in Honolulu one time and having trouble getting to sleep after his late night flight. He wound up wideawake at 3:00 a.m., so he got up and went to an all-night diner for a cup of coffee. All of a sudden, in came about eight women, laughing and talking loudly. Campolo concluded that these were streetwalkers, finishing up for the night. One, named Agnes, mentioned that the next day was her birthday. After the group left, Campolo got an idea. He said to the owner behind the counter, "Let's throw Agnes a birthday party. I'll come back tomorrow night with some decorations, and we'll surprise her with a birthday cake."

"That's a great idea," said the owner.

Twenty-four hours later, the diner was decorated with streamers and balloons and a large assortment of night people were gathered. When the prostitutes came in for their usual coffee, the shout went up, "Happy birthday Agnes!" The woman stood speechless as the singing began. Tears streamed down her face. The owner brought out the birthday cake with candles. "I'll cut the cake," he said.

But Agnes said, "Can I just keep the cake? I'll take it to my apartment, just for a couple of days. Please let me keep the cake."

So, out the door she fled, holding the cake as if it were the Holy Grail. There was an awkward silence for awhile when finally Campolo said, "Why don't we pray?" And he prayed for Agnes on her birthday, prayed that God would bring her peace and save her from all her trouble. "Hey, you didn't tell me you were a preacher," said the proprietor. "What kind of church do you preach at?"

Campolo thought for a moment. "I preach at the kind of church that throws birthday parties for whores at three-thirty in the morning."

What happened next was the most poignant moment of all. The man squinted at Campolo and said, "No...no, you don't. There is no church like that. I would join a church like that."

Turning Brown Into Green

I was visiting Martha at the nursing home, and as I walked down the hall, I could hear the moans and groans coming from the rooms. There was the familiar smell or urine. Patients were sitting in wheelchairs in the hall, staring at the floor. One of them—a lady who was wearing most of her breakfast—grabbed my arm as I passed and said, "Will you take me home?" *Brown.*

Our neighbor is about four weeks pregnant. I saw her in the grocery store. She looked worn out and anemic. I caught up with her and said, "Robin, are you okay?"

"Pray for me," she said, "I may lose the baby." *Brown.*

The United Methodist Women agreed to sponsor one of the rooms at the Women's Shelter. They would provide money and manpower to remodel one of the rooms that had been nearly destroyed by a leaky roof. The shelter is a haven for women—married and single—who have been beaten up by their husband or lover. Their self-esteem as well as their body—has been beaten into the ground. They are scared, homeless, and feeling helpless. *Brown.*

Jackie is a senior in high school. She is an honor student and plans to go to med school. She recently found out that she is pregnant. She has dropped out of school, and her parents are determined that Jackie will adopt the baby out. Jackie's future now is in the hands of others—in the hands of people who have no plans to go to med school and become a pediatrician. *Brown.*

People attend worship for many different reasons. Some attend out of habit—they have been coming to church for years. Some come for the fellowship—just to be around people. Some attend because it makes them feel good. Others enjoy the music. One elderly gentleman told me he comes to church to hear the children's sermon. But when all is said and done, there may be one reason that is more important than all the rest. I don't know of any other place—supermarket, the movie theater, the bowling alley, the local bar—where you can turn brown into *green.*

WAITING THE BAPTIST WAY

One thing all four gospels have in common when it comes to the Christmas story is John the Baptist. The more familiar portrait of the Baptist comes from Matthew and Luke—a wild-eyed prophet in camel's hair and leather, eating bugs soaked in honey. The fourth gospel offers no visual. In John's account, we have to deduce who he is from what he says—or rather does not say: Who are you? *I am not the Messiah.* Are you Elijah, then? *No.* Are you the prophet? *No.* Who are you, then? *I am a voice.* Why are you baptizing people if you are a nobody? *Because someone is coming after me who is a somebody.* I would not have wanted to be John. Here was a loner who knew God had something for him to do, who had a strong calling to do something spectacular—he just didn't know what it was. So, John must have had several conversations with God. You want me to do what? Be a voice? For whom? Where? In the wilderness? Who is going to hear me there? Who will care?

Until the moment arrived when John would know who, what, when, and where—his life was one long Advent, a waiting in the dark for the light, a waiting without knowing what you were waiting for. In other words, all John had to go on, the only thing that kept him on the lookout, that made the waiting tolerable, was a sense of the future.

What Advent teaches us, I think, is that our waiting for God to act is not a matter of entering into suspended animation. Our waiting is not nothing. It is something—a very big something—because people tend to be shaped by whatever it is they are waiting for.

Have you noticed that when you want something really bad, your whole life tends to rearrange itself around that thing? Maybe it's a baby. Maybe it's a house? A job. Leaving home. Getting a divorce. Waiting becomes an enemy rather than a friend. It is thought to serve no practical purpose at all. But there is no future, no promise without waiting. *How* we wait is huge!

As people of faith who are between advents—Jesus's first coming and his second—we need a theology for waiting, a heart for waiting. Maybe we can take some lessons from our kids who know how to wait for Christmas. It's not so much that they are patient about it—God knows they are anything but patient! But their waiting has some purpose to it. They learned somehow that Christmas is as much a journey as it is a destination. "He who has no Christmas in his heart," said the homeless man going through the dumpster, "will never find Christmas under a tree."

Wash Your Face

When I was in high school, I envied the Catholics during Lent because they were excused from school to attend mass on Ash Wednesday. When the students returned, they were "ashed" on their foreheads with the cross. I was both envious and puzzled. I was envious because they got out of school for a few hours. Why doesn't my church do something like that? And they walked around the halls of the school with this ashen cross on their forehead, now smudged but nonetheless noticeable a mile away. I was envious because I really believed that this cross of ashes served somehow as an amulet, and I had visions of these cross bearers being divinely protected. Bullies would give them a wide berth. They could walk into the path of a speeding car and not get hurt. They would be protected against colds and the flu. Who knows, maybe it gave them an edge while taking exams. For a short period of time, I wanted to be a Catholic.

I was puzzled because I didn't know why this was such a big thing with Catholics. I talked to my pastor about it, and he told me how imposition of ashes was a custom of the church since early Christianity; and it was a sign of repentance, humility, and fasting, acknowledging that without Jesus's sacrifice on the cross, we would be lost. I asked him why the Methodists don't do that, and his reply was, "We don't do that." And he had Scripture to back him up. Didn't Jesus say to his disciples, "When you fast, don't be like the hypocrites do who darken their faces just to get noticed. Instead, wash your face because it's not what other people see that's important but what God sees."

Well, that gave me some ammunition for dismissing both Catholics and their ashes because they didn't get it. It's not about appearances. When you pray, don't be like the hypocrites who love to pray in the village square so that everyone could see how sincere they were about their religion. And when you give, don't be like the hypocrites who like to flash their bills around as they put them in the offering plate. True giving is not about the gift being acknowledged—it's about giving without concern for acknowledgement.

So, I became a Catholic in reverse. In place of the cross of ashes, I wore this frown whenever I spotted hypocrites. I felt superior because I knew how to be righteous. I carried this frown around for some time until my wife got sick of it. Finally she said, "You need to go and wash your face."

PLANTING ONIONS AND POTATOES

For many people, it is extremely difficult to wrap their brain around the unconditional love of God. We embrace and celebrate it until it is applied to someone we don't like. I know what Jesus said, "Love your enemy. Love those who curse you." Is Jesus saying that we should reward the sinner and punish the saint? Is he saying that we should let our enemy off the hook? The thief breaks into the house, and while he is making his getaway, you shout, "Hey! You forgot my 65-inch Sony stereo with a 4K HDR processor X1 with smart capabilities and Bose sound." Is that what we are supposed to do?

Remember the scene at Jesus's Last Supper with his disciples? A woman enters and washes Jesus's feet with expensive nard. Judas objects, "Think of the poor and the hungry who could have been sheltered and fed from the sale of this perfume! Wasteful!" Think of the poinsettias that fill the chancel at Christmas. Think of the lilies that decorate the cross at Easter. Think of the communion plates and cups that were given as memorials. Think of the stained glass windows with the name of the donor etched in bright red at the bottom. We arrive for worship and are greeted with music from an organ that was financed by a local philanthropist. Think of the sterling candelabra, the padded pews, and the skylight in the ceiling, spreading sunlight on all the extravagance. "All a sinful waste!" says Judas, as well as those of us who know that there are people living in cardboard shanties beneath the underpass and children who end up in orphanages and women who end up in women's shelters.

I sing in a barbershop chorus, and every Valentine's Day, a group of quartets deliver singing valentines. I sing in one of those quartets, and for $30, we deliver a rose, a helium filled balloon, and two love songs. We were on our way to fill a request from a young wife to her husband who was unemployed. The only income coming in was from her work as a house cleaner and seamstress. They had to move into a rundown rental in an area of the city called "Dump Town." When we arrived we had to be careful, lest we fall through the porch. The screen door was attached with wire and duct tape. We knocked on the door, and the husband answered. He had been feeding their fourteen-month-old baby. We told him who we were and why we were there. The room was filled with the foul odor of kerosene from the heater in the corner. We delivered the rose and balloon and sang, "Let Me Call You Sweetheart" and "Sweet Roses of Morn." The man was in tears when we left. One of my quartet buddies said, "I don't get it. She spends $30 on a balloon that will soon sag to the floor, a rose that will wilt in three days, and a couple of songs! She could have bought a month's supply of diapers for $30! Kinda wasteful, isn't it?"

Recall the trilogy of lost parables in Luke 15. A shepherd had a hundred sheep, and one wandered off into the wilderness. The shepherd, leaving the nine-nine behind, goes in search of the one that was lost. Risk the safety of the ninety-nine to recover the one? A sensible businessman would say, "Forget it and cut your losses." How much is one sheep worth, anyway?

A woman has ten coins, and in the business of the day, she carelessly loses one of the coins. She crawls on her hands and knees in search of that one coin, and when she finds it, she calls in the other women in the neighborhood and throws a party to celebrate. This is what gets me. The celebration probably cost more than what the one coin was worth!

A man had two sons, the younger one was itching to go out on his own. He demands that his father give him his inheritance, something that does not occur until the father dies. In other words, he wishes that his father was dead. Oddly enough, the father gives the younger son what he wants, and the young boy goes off to a faraway place where only Gentiles live and parties like a freshman in college.

When the boy has spent everything on booze and bad women and can no longer support himself, he decides to return home where he can get three squares a day and a roof over his head.

The problem is, because of his rebellion—according to ancient mid-eastern custom—the father will whip him to make him an example to all the other would-be young deserters and will, indeed, force him into servitude in order to pay back all the he has wasted. Justice demands it, and so do the villagers. But as the boy draws near the village, the father runs out to meet him, hugs, and kisses him and—get this—the father throws a party to welcome him home instead of serving him the sharp end of a whip. How much is a person worth?

You see what I mean. Not only is all of this celebrating and killing the fatted calf wasteful, but it goes against everything we have been taught about fairness and justice. We are expected to pay for our mistakes and suffer the consequences of our actions. We don't like to see people getting away with anything. And when the lost ones get off scot free, the villagers in our churches and in our neighborhoods will strongly object to, what appears to be, cheap grace. The problem is no one taught you or me about the waste of love, the extravagance of God, "grace upon grace" as Paul would put it. There is one thing God is not—he is not cheap! We haven't yet learned that it is okay to plant roses instead of onions and potatoes. It's okay.

WHAT AM I PRAYING FOR?

I find prayer to be very confusing—I always have. Let me try to explain. A few years ago, the New Yorker magazine carried a cartoon depicting a child dragging his Teddy bear up the stairs. He turns to his parents sitting in the living room and says, "I'm going to bed now to say my prayers. Anybody want anything?" Do you want a new job? Pray. Do you want a baby? Pray? Do you want to get rid of your cold? Pray. Do you want to pass algebra? Pray. Do you want it to rain? Pray. Do you want it to stop raining? Pray. Paul says, "Pray without ceasing." Okay, Paul, but you are a saint. What if you are just one of those believers who never gets above a two or a three on the *Christian Perfection* scale?

In ancient times, the Jews believed that you were especially devout if you prayed three times a day—morning, noon, and night. That's fine if you are an organized person and disciplined, and then there are all of those rules—written and unwritten about prayer—you should pray for needs, but not desires. You should pray only when your heart is right, otherwise your prayer is unworthy. Is it okay to pray that you win the lottery? Is it okay to pray for money? For a new car? To win a ball game? To find a boyfriend? To find the ring you lost when you were gardening? Don't pray when you are angry. Don't pray when you are tired. And we haven't even discussed what prayer is. Is it a red phone to God? Is it words and conversation? How do you know you are praying and not just mumbling to yourself?

It helps to look at what Jesus had to say. In his Sermon on the Mount in Matthew, he says, "When you pray, don't be like the hypocrites who love to stand and pray in the synagogues and street corners." In other words, don't use prayer as an attention getter, to impress others. "Instead," says Jesus, "pray in your closet. That way, you will be praying to God instead of to the brown-nosers. And don't heap empty phrases one on top of the other when you pray." In other words, don't rattle on and on, thinking that prayer is an acceptance speech.

I know that sometimes we cannot find the words to express what we want, and so we turn to formal prayers like the Lord's Prayer and "God is great, God is good, thank you for this food, Amen"—to get it said. The thing is, God wants to hear what we do not want to say and wants to hear what we cannot say. In other words, God wants to listen to our heart.

I am not always conscious of my prayers because my thoughts about God and my family, God and my work, God and my fears get mixed together. What I mean is, God and I have this understand-ing—that I love him more than life, and I don't always say what I mean and mean what I say; and besides, every conversation I have with others and with myself is within earshot of God, so maybe I'm praying even when I don't think I'm praying.

Maybe prayer is just a way of trying to live out my life in a way that makes God smile. So, unless I have something very, very specific to bring to God in a formal way, I am aware that God is listening in on all my conversations—and God has a way of figuring out which ones need the most attention—and which ones are just talking. It's a good thing that God can do that because even when I consciously know that I am praying, I don't always get it right. Yes, I know. I'm one confused prayer-er.

What's Normal?

"For there is no distinction, since all have sinned and have fallen short..." My usual take on this observation from Paul in his Roman letter is that no one is perfect. I still think that's true. But after meditating on this idea for a while, I have come up with another idea. Whether Paul had this in mind or not—who knows. But what if Paul is also saying, "No one is normal" and "everybody is weird." John Ortberg, in his book, *Everybody's Normal Til You Get To Know Them*, makes this same observation. "We all want to look normal, to think of ourselves as normal, but the writers of Scripture insist that no one is 'totally normal'—at least not as God defines normal." The Bible is loaded with a cast of characters who come nowhere near the Walton's on Walton's Mountain.

Everybody's weird. We tend to measure everyone by some kind of whacky standard for "normal." No one really knows where this standard came from, nor do we know precisely how it works. All we know is that if it quacks like a duck, walks like a duck, looks like a duck—it must be a duck. And when we use this standard to measure our friends and our enemies, we get it wrong most of the time. Because everybody is weird. Everybody is operating from a set of genes different from ours. The only thing that is predictable when it comes to human nature is that it is unpredictable.

Why is this so important? Because the life and health of the faith community is at stake. Because we are so often disappointed in those who do not measure up, who walk, talk, and look differently than they are supposed to as Christians. And when they demonstrate *weirdness,* we either separate ourselves from them or judge them harshly.

In his chapter, "The Porcupine Dilemma," Ortberg says that porcupines have two methods for dealing with relationships: withdrawal and attack. Most pastors are familiar with this strategy on the part of those who have been hurt or otherwise disappointed by what the pastor or a church member did or did not do. Like the porcupine, we do one of two things—we either drop out of sight and become truant from worship, or we pull out our arsenal of sharp, barbed quills and let go.

May I suggest that the next time you are in conflict with someone in the faith community, you resist being a porcupine. I know that this is not "normal," and goes against our instincts to fight or flight—but there is more than our feelings at stake. There is also the shalom of the faith community. So, how about doing something that is not normal? How about saying to your fellow brother or sister in Christ—"can we talk?"

Why Can't We Just Get Along?

I pulled into a gas station to gas up. Two pumps to my left were two men arguing. One was in the car and the other outside the car on the driver's side, window rolled down. I couldn't quite make out what they were arguing about, but by the animation and hand gestures, I knew they weren't talking sports. I went about pumping gas with one ear cocked. Then, I heard the man standing outside the car scream at the other, "If you really knew me, you wouldn't have said that about me," and he walked away.

You will recall back in 1991, Rodney King was speeding on a California highway and was pulled over by a police cruiser. Two officers ordered King and two others in the car to get out. In the process, King and his friends were severely beaten with nightsticks by the officers as well as two other officers who had arrived on the scene. The four officers were charged with assault with a deadly weapon but were acquitted. The acquittals led to the 1992 Los Angeles riots when fifty-three people were killed and two thousand injured. Later, in an interview, King said to reporters, "Why can't we just learn to get along?"

An article in Psychology Today asserted that humans are 98 percent emotional and only 2 percent rational. That goes a long way in helping to explain why we can't get along. But I am going back to the gas station and the comment, "If you really knew me, you wouldn't have said that about me." I think an essential element in demonstrating hostility and ill will toward another is distance. Distance is required to criticize and dehumanize another person. They have to remain strangers. "Did you see the way he limps? Look at her nose—

why doesn't she get a nose job? Does she realize how fat she is—why doesn't she lose weight? Did you see how messy their house was? No one has to live that way!"

The people who do not notice the crooked nose, the limp, and the extra weight in the caboose are family members and friends because there is no distance. What might happen if we knew that the man with the limp was a soldier returning from Afghanistan? What would happen if we knew that the woman's crooked nose was the result of spousal abuse? What would happen if we knew that this woman's obesity is the result of hormonal irregularities? Would knowing all of this make a difference?

It might. But there are certain advantages to having enemies or acquaintances who are unpolished, irregular, or otherwise different than we are—they serve as scapegoats for our anger, our low self-esteem, and our own irregularities. Everyone needs an enemy or two. So, in order to preserve this defense mechanism, we have to maintain our distance, for sure as the sun rises in the morning, if you get to know your enemy things won't be the same. Pretty soon, you will be having lunch with the guy with the limp, and he will tell you about how he lost his lower leg stepping on an IED. And you will tell him about the hell you went through in Vietnam and how your wife took up with another man while you were gone. And pretty soon something happens you weren't ready for—you realize that you don't need an enemy after all. What you needed all along was someone to love and be loved in return.

You Won't See Their Halos

As a cancer patient, my wife completed a series of chemo treatments, and I spent some time with her while the IV was sending the life-saving chemicals into her veins. I watched as the nurses went about the business of healing and comforting. Who are these people? Why do they do this? *These nurses are saints,* I thought. No, in fact, they are angels. I remembered from the Greek I learned some time ago that the word angel comes from the Greek word, "euangelion." It gets translated "messenger." That's where our words, "evangelical" and "angel," come from. Recall what brought the news to the world that a Savior was born—angels. These are not simply nurses. They are not just employees of the center. But I'll wager that missing in their job descriptions is the word, "angel." How else can you describe someone whose hands and heart bring such healing and comfort?

Think about it. Isn't this the way God performs his healing miracles, through caring and compassionate men and women dedicated to the art of healing? Why is it any less a miracle when God uses human hands to do the healing?

I have long ago given up the idea that angels are supernatural beings with wings and a halo. In the truest sense of the word, angels are messengers sent from God to heal and to comfort.

I remember reading about a Sunday school teacher named Miss Hutchison who, one day, was teaching about the miracles of Jesus. One little girl asked, "Miss Hutchison, do you really think that Jesus had a halo like you see in all the pictures of him?"

"Well," she said, "have you ever seen someone whose face was all radiant with sunshine?"

The girl replied, "Yes, you, Miss Hutchison."

Another little girl chimed in, "I spent a week with Miss Hutchison while my mother was away, and I never saw her halo."

You walk into the Cancer Center, and you will see all these angels at work—you just won't see their halos.

ABOUT THE AUTHOR

Ted Cole is a retired pastor, having served United Methodist churches for over forty years. He earned his bachelor's degree at Allegheny College in Meadville, Pennsylvania, his master of divinity at Pittsburgh Theological Seminary, and his doctor of ministry at Pittsburgh Theological Seminary. Ted has written a number of short faith-related articles for church newsletters and local newspapers. He presently resides in Mill Village, Pennsylvania, in Erie County and is active in an area United Methodist Church as a Bible teacher.